10K
& 5K

RUNNING,
TRAINING
& RACING

THE RUNNING PYRAMID

By DAVID HOLT

31 MINUTE 10K &
15 MINUTE 5K

Library of Congress Catalog Card Number 98-96605
Holt, David
  10K & 5K Running, Training & Racing: The Running Pyramid, by David Holt.
  Includes index and photos.
  1. Running-Training 2. Running-Jogging 3.Self-help running 4. Exercise-Aerobic
  796.42-dc20
ISBN 0-9658897-1-8

Chapter	CONTENTS	Page

The Training Advice

The Training Schedules

First Printing November 1998
     10 9 8 7 6 5 4 3 2 1

First there was the food pyramid. Now comes the running pyramid. This logical book brings you 180 pages of expert advice on how to form your own training pyramid for successful 5K and 10K running, and how to avoid too much speedwork or too many slow miles which can ruin your racing.

In 10K & 5K Running, Training and Racing David sticks to his best distances. The English club system, and prudent training through all five phases of the Running Pyramid, helped David to achieve 31:16 for 10,000 meters (5:02 miles) and 15:18 for 5,000 meters.
David ran 3,000 miles a year--the most he could do while remaining injury free for 11 consecutive years. He has run well over 300 races on track, road and cross-country. David has contributed to Runner's World and Running Times, and writes a monthly running feature for the Internet's "Transition Times".

Special thanks to Meg Barbour, John Brennand, Nancy Caponi, Greg Horner, Terry Howell, Carol Knox, Jim Knox, Nancy Madrigal, Dave Scott, Kevin Young.

Other Books by DAVID HOLT.
RUNNING DIALOGUE is a humorous look at How To Train from the 5K to the Marathon, for beginner to expert. It includes extensive injury prevention and treatment sections plus nutrition advice and essays.

David Holt is a Registered Nurse, with a Diploma in Orthopedic Nursing, who runs, works, writes and lives in Santa Barbara, California.

Peaking
VO2 Max Intervals
Anaerobic Threshold
Hills and Strength Training

CHAPTER ONE

BUILDING BASE MILEAGE & FARTLEK

Why Race 5,000 meters?

Bragging rights. To non-runners, racing 3.1 miles is as distant as a marathon.

It's short, it's fast, and 5,000 meters is over very quickly. It requires modest mileage.

However, a 15-20 minute race is hardly a sprint.

You will still need to run the same mileage which you would do for 10K training.

So why run 5Ks anyway?

You will need 5,000s to prepare yourself for the 10K.

Why Race 10,000 meters?

First, it's a slower, more comfortable pace than the 5,000 meters. 8 to 12 seconds per mile slower makes this distance a joy. You can and should still train at 5K pace; you should still race some 5Ks; perhaps one third of your races will be at 5,000 meters. You don't have to give up those big events at the ocean where you rub shoulders with the elite.

Second, you can rectify mistakes. Too fast or too slow in the first mile...don't worry too much...you have 5.2 miles to adjust.

Third, it hurts less during the race--compared to the 5,000 meters. It hurts less after the race--compared to the marathon. If you've ever raced a marathon up to your fitness level, you know about pain: both during and after the marathon. Your walking can entertain friends for days after a marathon.

Fourth, unless your name is Doug, you can't race many marathons. 10-20 per decade is most peoples limit. You can *run* that many 10Ks each year.

Fifth, your longest run each week is not very long!

Successful 10K and 5K training requires a commitment to mileage and endurance training--only with this solid base should you enter the three phases of speed training. Maintain form during the mileage phase with strides, fartlek and intervals, but increase your mileage to whatever level your body or psyche can handle. Your mileage limit may be physical or mental.

Each run must have a purpose--aim to improve your running biomechanics AND your aerobic ability during base training. Training increases muscle size and strength; it strengthens tendons, ligaments and bones.

Use cross training and weight training for additional strength, but keep the cross training relevant to your running muscles and running motion--don't bulk up; use many reps at modest resistance in weight training.

10K and 5K Training: Mileage Base for Strength Endurance.

The typical suggestions in training books or magazines suggest 60-80 mile weeks for marathon racing, 50 mile weeks for the half marathon, 40 miles for 10K racing, and 30 miles for the 5K. But how do you build an aerobic base on 30-40 miles per week? At all these distances, you need a 15 mile distance run most weeks to build stamina, aerobic pathways, mitochondria, red blood cells and Myoglobin. Long runs also prepare you for the aerobic strides, VO2 max enhancing intervals, and threshold pace training, which you will do in the next three phases.

To race well at any distance, then, you need to put in long runs, and decent mileage. How long should your long run be?

Top British coach, and frequent contributor to the British Athletic magazines, Frank Horwill, says that "Physiologists believe steady runs should be at least 35 minutes to get a training effect."

Horwill continues, "Exercise physiologist David Costill reports the volume of steady running alone at 80 percent VO2 max improves fitness by as much as 12 percent to 80 miles per week. After that, there is very little return for the mileage expended. A good way of building to this volume is to add 5 minutes per day per week to the running. A 35 minute per day runner will reach 70 minutes after seven weeks."

What about the longest run of the week?

Not more than one third of your total weekly miles--unless that would involve running less than eight miles. The 30 per week person could run a 10 miler each week. Reach 45 per week and you'll be able to handle the 15 miler recommended for most runners hoping to race well at 5 and 10K. Hit 60 per week though, and your long run would be only 25 percent of the weekly training!

Speedwork Too.

This commitment to mileage and endurance training need not neglect strides, fartlek and your current interval training--which should sustain and possibly improve your running form. If you've been racing predominantly 5Ks, don't give up your legspeed in this strength phase. Maintain your hard won running form at speed. If you've been running marathons without any speedwork, take note of the fartlek section coming up.

The increased mileage may take you close to your injury threshold...the point where you are close to injury; or the decisive mileage ceiling could be the amount you can handle mentally. It may only be 30 miles; it could be 60 or 90.

Increase mileage by about 10 percent per week on average, until you reach your unique limit, or if you are lucky, your goal.

If you feel radical, or if you've had a high mileage phase in the past, you could add ten miles per week for two weeks...then consolidate for a week or two before increasing again. For instance, if you ran 60 miles per week last year, but you've been enjoying a low-key 35 miles for several months, jumping back to 55 miles over two weeks should not strain your already sound physique. Adding 10 percent per week would require five weeks to reach fifty-five miles. Those runners entering higher mileage for the first time should practice prudence--stay with the 10 percent guide.

You can add a few minutes to each run, or you can add half a mile at a time--the net result is the same: increased mileage.

Seek Variety.

The person who was on low mileage training while racing short distances may have problems coping with boredom during high mileage.

Use your brain to plan, then use it again while running, and you'll rarely be bored. Some people think all running is boring, yet you're rarely stuck in a gym on a motorized belt to nowhere. Even if you do run on a treadmill occasionally, you have other athletes in the room to watch or amuse yourself with--their antics can entertain for hours. Just don't get involved with the silliness of people competing for exercise equipment.

Mostly though, you are going somewhere; most of your running will be outside. Make the higher mileage more fun by using different training areas--parks, trails, quiet streets and bike paths all have their attractions. Give way to horse riders and cyclists as appropriate, soak up the scenery, and think about your form.

Those of you coming down from the marathon can still run your high mileage, but the longest run need only be 15 miles--which will leave you fresher in the rest of the week for fast running.

Maintain Form during High Mileage.
As former University of Florida coach and author Roy Benson understates, "Run in a fairly straight line for running efficiency."

Running Economy and Efficiency.

Let your ankles roll as you glide along.

Feet should be moving backwards when they land on the ground--ready to propel you forward.

Land with a slightly bent knee, as if onto eggshells. A soft footfall with flexed knee reduces the pounding.

Land on the outer edge of the heel or mid-foot, then roll inwards to a neutral position as you move toward push-off.

Push yourself forward powerfully with the calf muscles: By extending the trail leg to its full length, and
    pushing off from the end of your toes.

Run upright; run tall. Some say a one percent forward lean helps! Bring the hips forward.

Make your feet hug the buttocks as they swing through on each stride. Whip those feet through.

Practice butt kicks or high heels as strides; run some high knees exercises. Think legspeed when you do these drills. Five of each for 50 meters will suffice.

> Keep your hands loose and relaxed. A clenched fist transfers its tension to the shoulders. Save the energy for your leg muscles by keeping the fingers lightly curled.

Chapter 1: Mileage Base & Fartlek.

Keep your arms quite low; move them in rhythm with your legs: move them just enough to stop your shoulders rolling. This should stop your head from rolling too.

But don't: Land daintily on the toes, or with a locked knee, or copy sprinters.

Use these pointers as a guide to help you run smoothly--avoid wasteful, unneeded motions because oxygen efficiency is dependent upon running efficiency.

Keep "economy enhancing speedwork" in your weekly schedule while you increase mileage, but keep most of the new mileage at about 70 percent of your maximum heartrate. Maintain the new "higher mileage" for at least eight weeks before working through phases two to five of 10K and 5K training.

Don't follow someone else's training program; develop a mix which is appropriate to you. If two twelve mile runs a week suits you better than one run of fifteen, don't be ashamed. Fifteens are not for everyone. Though it is the long run of choice for many top runners.

One way to allocate 49-56 miles:
Day one...15 miles
Day two...6 miles
Day three...5 miles--include 20 gentle strides--not sprints
Day four...10 miles
Day five...7 miles--including three miles of fartlek
Day six...3 miles or rest
Day seven...6-9 miles...details page 150.

Beginners, Intermediate and Experienced Runners. Or,

Serious, Moderate and High Intensity Runners.

With variations of course, there are three main intensities of training. The three types are represented at all weekly mileage levels. There are high intensity trainers who run 30 miles per week, and lower intensity runners who enjoy 60 per week.

High intensity runners will run fast about three times per week. Most high intensity trainers will do a quality fast session on day 7 of the above schedule, then run off the effects during the long run on the following day. They have probably been running for several years and will do a session which is familiar to them on day 7--they'll work at improving form, speed and strength on days 1, 3 and 5. Day seven might involve alternating five miles of 400s or quarters at 5K to 10K pace; with five times one mile at 15K pace; with 800 meter reps at 10K pace; with hill repeats.

If you have been used to running them, you can still run anaerobic threshold, VO2 max or hill sessions during base build-up, but do keep the emphasis on increasing your base. See the detailed schedule options starting at Chapter Seven.

The moderate intensity runner may have just as much running experience as the high intensity person, but choose to run hard twice a week. Note the absence of the adjective "only" before twice in the last sentence. For many runners, two speed running sessions per week is the perfect scheme to achieve fast and satisfying races. Separate speed running days with one or two easy days.

Chapter 1: Mileage Base & Fartlek.

The serious runner may train at speed once per week. In the early weeks, your long run may feel quite harsh...it can feel like a hard run. Keep the pace to 60 percent of your maximum heartrate (HR) until it begins to feel easy to you. Most writers would call this the novice or beginner group, and shun speedwork. This authors philosophy is that the people who benefit most from speedwork *are* the novices. Speedwork improves your running form and efficiency. One fartlek session per week can bring the same benefit as half of your other mileage. There are no recreational runners in 10K and 5K training and racing. When running one speed session each week, you're at least a serious runner; many runners in this group have been training for years.

The training levels then are:
High intensity; Moderate intensity; and,
Serious runners.
At all three levels, the long run is crucial.

Your Mileage Base Will:

Add muscle strength or endurance--more on this in Chapter Two.

Increase the size and number of your mitochondria, which are the engines of oxygen use in the muscles.

Don't start your runs too fast. Your legs get tired, and the muscles fill up with lactic acid--the wastes of anaerobic running. Your running action becomes labored. You'll be forced to slow down...which is demoralizing. Start runs at 60 percent of maximum HR.

Increase Myoglobin within the cell, which delivers oxygen to the mitochondria.

Expand your capillary network, to bring in nutrients and excrete waste products.

Enlarge the chamber size and stroke volume of your heart--increasing the quantity of blood pumped out with each heart contraction.

Increase the size and number of red blood cells (RBCs)--which bring oxygen to your muscle cells.

Increase your blood volume--which takes most of the carbon dioxide to your lungs for excretion. Your RBCs get diluted, so you may appear anemic on blood tests.

Build bigger muscle fibers...in the heart and in the running muscles.

Develop strength endurance in your diaphragm and intercostal muscles, allowing you to breathe in deeper, more often, more forcefully.

The net result is an enhanced capacity to take in and distribute oxygen.

The more of the above factors which you improve with training, the more you will amplify your aerobic ability, or your maximum oxygen uptake capacity--VO2 max.

Running is simple and progressive: You train moderately hard, then take a rest. You rest regularly each week and each month.

Some people run 10 miles at 70 percent max HR on a rest day; other people run 3 miles for the rest day. Take a rest week every three to four weeks; it should be about 40 percent fewer miles than your normal training week.

The Right Speed.

The high mileage build-up for racing 10K and 5K should not be a slow mileage build-up. Run long slow distance (LSD) above 60 percent of maximum heartrate. Stay close to 60 percent in the early runs; once you've done several long ones, guarantee that your cardiopulmonary system is adequately stimulated by running at 70 percent.

How do you know what your maximum heartrate is?

If you are new to running, or to steady sustained exercise, subtract your age from 220.

Once you have run eight miles a few times, and half a dozen fartlek sessions, you'll be ready for a heartrate test. Warm-up with about two miles at gentle pace. After stretching, run three or four strides of about 100 meters. Then, run all-out for about 90 seconds. If you've been exercising for several years, do this up a slight hill. After a rest, run all-out again for 90 seconds, but pace yourself to reach exhaustion at 90 seconds. If you reach exhaustion at 60 seconds, you'll be running slower at 90 seconds--the lower reading from the heartrate test will mislead you into a lower pace (at which) to run your steady runs. Check your pulse for ten seconds--multiply by six. Or read your heartrate monitor if you use one. The number will either be your maximum heartrate (HR), or the maximum level at which your body or pain threshold allows you to exercise.

Sixty to 70 percent of your maximum HR should represent a pace at which you can talk easily in 8-10 word sentences. You should not be huffing and puffing 2-3 word responses--that comes in Chapter Three.

Fartlek during Base Training.

If you're new to fast running, you only need to start with 6-8 gentle strides. As the English would say, "Any twerp can sprint 50 meters to catch a bus." If the twerp doesn't have a heart attack, said person could sprint again in a month or two! A 100 meter stride or build-up is much slower than an all out sprint. This is supposed to be gentle training...not a straining of muscles. Build to two miles of gentle speedplay at one minute per mile faster than your steady run pace; gradually increase the speed to half marathon race pace. This minimal fast running will improve your running form; it avoids junk miles.

When you become used to the increased mileage, you can bring the last few strides down to 10K speed. Over the course of a year, by changing one stride a month to this pace, most of the speedplay can become 10K race pace. As you will see in phases three and four, the preferred paces are 15K and 5K speed.

During this first phase though, you can be generic, 10K pace is a safe goal.

According to coach Benson, "Aerobic speedwork improves flexibility, strength and coordination."

Speedplay or fartlek is a controlled OR uncontrolled system to accomplish quality running and speedwork. It can be a "run fast when you feel like it" session, or you can have a set plan--perhaps 20 efforts of 200 to 300 meters. Another day, you might plan 8 half mile efforts. Or, use a combination of the two. Use sections of your run with the safest footing, or least traffic, or most mud, or enjoyable slope; then run at easy pace to recover.

Fartlek is:

a great way to recover after long runs;
quality aerobic conditioning speedwork;
an ideal extra session during a high mileage build-up;
a great anti-aging device for masters' running:
fartlek is a great playtool.
However intense your running is, most distance running
for the 5K and 10K should still be fun.

When playing, that is running, use fartlek training for:

Post Long Distance Run Recovery.

After the longest run of the week, fartlek brings pep back
to your legs...gently. Two days post long run, do 100 to
400 meter striders over varying terrain, at different
speeds or paces.

A soft surface is best for fartlek. This fartlek will
prepare you for the more formal, or serious speedwork 4
days after your long run.

Quality Aerobic Conditioning.

All distance running helps your aerobic conditioning.
However, fartlek's speedplay brings in those reluctant
fast twitch muscle fibers. Fire up the fast twitchers--get
the entire muscle into action.

Most 10K runners possess predominantly slow twitch
muscle fibers; 5K specialists possess more fast twitch
fibers. All these runners need to put their muscles
through a full range of motion at least twice a week to
maintain good running form, while getting full use from
the fast fibers.

Runners with more fast twitch fibers usually find speed training easy--they are natural speed-meisters. You should still do the fartlek, but the strides must not be sprints. Your goal is to teach these short work duration fibers to work at submaximal capacity for a significant time period...namely, the 30 to 40 minutes which it takes to race a 10K. Long fartlek sessions at modest pace, and high mileage with long runs will improve the endurance of these fast twitch fibers.

When to do Fartlek Running.

You can do these gentle fartlek sessions the evening after a long distance run, (unless it was longer, or faster than you've been used to); or the morning of the day on which you plan to run miles of track repeats. The fartlek will make you feel looser in both situations. Feeling looser after a long run, or looser before a track workout, a gentle fartlek run works both ways.

Leg Strength and Masters Anti-aging.

Fartlek keeps your legs strong as you go through the masters age groups--as does all speed training. Use it to gain or maintain leg strength at all ages.

Speedplay also stimulates endorphin production inside your body for healing and health. The endorphins make us feel good too--the endorphin produced by our body is more potent than morphine.

Experiment at speed. See how much easier, (or harder) it is to run at a certain pace with higher knees, or short rapid strides, or a ground hugging running style.

18

Former Miler or 5,000 Runner?

Keep your legspeed (cadence) with 30-90 second efforts.

Play around with your knee lift and stride length.

Push off from the toes--you can still enjoy the speed.

Run some longer efforts too--a nice relaxed tempo for 3-7 minutes--feel the power in your legs from your new mileage base. However, don't run all-out.

Coming up from the Marathon: (some
runners think 5K and 10K is the highest form of racing).

Rarely ran speedwork in your marathon preparation? Be gentle with your first few fartleks. Run fartlek once a week for four weeks, then twice a week for at least four more weeks before moving on to Chapter Two.

Those who did speedwork in their marathon preparation will not have a problem with fartlek. Just run a variety of distances and paces.

If you're adding a four mile run each month to increase training from 60 to 80 miles per week, the first, third and fifth month's additional run could be fartlek.

Recreational runners (sometimes called joggers), will find fartlek the most humane way to incorporate speedwork into their 10 to 20 miles a week.

When running while tired toward the end of a long run, or the last few efforts during a fartlek session, don't develop poor technique. Keep your shoulders loose; keep your arms down; don't lean too much; and, keep control of your running form.

Gather your mental resources and run four more strides to practice good form with fatigued muscles.

Fartlek Pace.

Use appropriate running pace and distances for a more formal session.

Use long reps at 15K pace for anaerobic threshold training, mixed with long reps at 5K pace for VO2 Max training; or do short efforts at either pace.

If you want a hard training session, run the same amount of time at fast pace that you would run in an interval or tempo session. Use a different section of the forest or park for each effort. Let perceived intensity and breathing guide your speed.

One of the best Runner's World magazine articles a few years ago was a series of favorite workouts which the elite did when they only had 40 minutes to train. Half of them said a fartlek session was the way to go. The amusing part was that most of these runners then described a repetition or interval session. Most simply ran six times half a mile or something similar. Should you call 6 x 800 meters a fartlek session?

True fartlek means a variety of distances. If you want to time yourself between two landmarks close to the beginning of the session, and again towards the end of the session, go ahead. Or run two times a set distance for pace judgment in the middle part. But do keep most of your fartlek free flowing.

Training for the 10K and 5K requires building up the individual muscle cells...the sarcomeres. The long run and high mileage are vital factors in training the Muscle Fiber Unit.

Sarcomere--Muscle Contraction Unit.

The sarcomere is the contractile unit of muscle: It's an all or nothing situation. The sarcolemma (the nerve), either fire the sarcomere to contract or it doesn't. It is just like an electric switch, either on or off. The total amount of a muscle's contractile power is dependent upon how many of your sarcomere contract at one time, and how long it takes before they can contract again.

Your Mileage Training will:

Boost the number of sarcomere which can contract at one time, and,

Increase the frequency at which they can contract.

Achieve these and you will be able to run fast for a longer distance.

Each sarcomere, or muscle contraction unit, is joined indirectly to bone. The transition of muscle to tendon--the so called Muscle-Tendon unit--is very susceptible to injury.

Increase training sensibly to keep these millions of tiny units intact.

Sarcomere or Muscle Protection.

Don't make sudden changes to your training schedule.
Add a mile or two to your long run every two weeks.
Add half a mile to your speed session every two weeks.
Work within the limits of YOUR body.
Stretch regularly and slowly.

Flexibility, long muscles, will make your running easier and reduce your injury risk.

The late Dr. George Sheehan, who wrote for Runner's World, had his magic six.

Podiatrist and extensive Internet writer Dr. Pribut has his magic 6 plus two.

I've extracted the best and basic for you--it may surprise you to see three are not for the legs. The back and shoulder are crucial to comfortable running.

For ego sake, lets call them:

Holt's Seven Stretches:

Calf and Achilles...Wall Push-Up: Pribut's version stretches one leg at a time. Stand with the rear foot approximately two to three feet from the wall. The rear leg should be straight, the front leg bent, and your hands touch the wall--feet point straight ahead, heels are on the ground. Hold for 10 seconds, switch legs, repeat 10 times.

Hamstring Stretch: Straighten one leg, place it with the knee locked on a sturdy support about 1-2 feet high. Bend your body and bring your head towards the leg. Hold this position for 10 seconds. Switch sides, repeat 10 times.

Quadriceps Stretch: Lie on your belly, or stand tall. Bring your right foot up towards your buttock, clasp the ankle with either hand and pull until you feel the quads are at their limit. Hold and repeat 5 times. Switch sides.

Chapter 1: Mileage Base & Fartlek.

Back. The Knee Clasp: Lie on your back. Bring both knees to your chest. Hold for 10 seconds. Repeat 5 times. This stretches the hamstrings and lower back.

I-T Band. Same position as above. Bring one knee up; pull the knee across your abdomen toward your shoulder.

Two for the Back and Abdomen.

Chest Push-Up: Lie belly down with your abdomen pressed flat on the floor. Place your hands beneath your shoulders. Push your chest up with your arms and hold for 10 seconds. Repeat 5 times.

Backward Stretch: While standing straight, place the palms of your hands against the small of your back. Tighten your buttocks and bend backwards. Hold for 10 seconds, relax, repeat 5 times.

Muscle efficiency is stimulated and improved by running long, but also by quality running such as fartlek and hill training. Weight and cross training play a role in making muscle cells more efficient, provided your extra muscle bulk does not adversely effect your running form. See page 49 for weight training.

A Fartlek question.

Matt, a Physical Training Instructor in New Zealand was to study one of the major energy systems and a training method. His interest was Fartlek Training to improve VO2 Max, or the maximum amount of oxygen that an exerciser can process; or aerobic capacity.

"The problem," says Matt, "is that fartlek is both anaerobic and aerobic, and my instructors argue that my aim is to improve VO2 Max--so what is the point of training in the anaerobic system. A fair point I guess, but I'm interested in finding out the effects of anaerobic work on the aerobic system during exercise and recovery (as is the nature of fartlek training)."

Matt went on to say he might modify fartlek training so that his subjects are always working in the aerobic system. His aim would be "aerobically powered fartlek training to improve VO2 Max."

Working predominantly the aerobic or the anaerobic system is dependent on which lengths and paces you concentrate your fartlek efforts upon. You can do all fartlek at anaerobic threshold or all at VO2 max by running at 15K or 2 mile pace respectively. Whichever pace you train at, you'll also stimulate the other system.

As I said above, all running does improve both systems--we can only emphasize a particular system.

Which is what Matt did, by having his subjects run at 5K pace.

You may take 10 weeks to reach your mileage goal. During these 10 weeks you should be bringing in the fartlek running. Run another eight weeks at high mileage with your full fartlek session and you'll be ready to race.

Call me radical, but you don't need to work through all five phases of 10K and 5K training to race well. Drop your mileage by 25 percent one week in four to rest up for a race. You can also race at related distances. Up to the half marathon if you are running 40 miles or more per week; 3K and 8K or 5 miles are great distances too. Enjoy the race day thrills and sensations a couple times before entering your strength training phase with Chapter Two.

Peak
Intervals
at VO2 Max
Anaerobic Threshold

CHAPTER TWO

HILLS AND STRENGTH TRAINING

You've done Base Mileage and Fartlek.

You can race successfully at 5 and 10 kilometers by doing the next three phases (Chapter Two to Chapter Four) in any order. Many coaches, and this writer, believe hill or strength training should follow the initial mileage build-up. If you prefer anaerobic threshold or VO2 max training first, work through the sessions from Chapter Three and Four respectively before returning to hill training. The best results, runners with the fastest times, train using all three types of running.

You should have raced at least two 5Ks and two 10Ks by now, so whatever intensity you train at, you have some idea what these races entail.

Now, whether you've come straight from phase one, or back from phase four, lets ease this muscle strengthener into your 5K and 10K running schedule. After all, distance runners gain muscle strength, stronger hearts and better knee lift with hill repeats.

Hill Running Develops the Neurological Pathways Needed for Fast Running.

Middle and long distance runners need strength and legspeed from hill repeats or other resistance training. Top 5,000 meter runners can be milers who do not race at 10K or specialists at 10K. Top 10K racers are at the crossroads of running: they can be sub 3:50 milers or sub 2:08 marathoners. They, and you, have perhaps the most to gain from doing some form of resistance training--we'll look at other options later--running hills is the simplest form of resistance training.

Provided you stayed at phase one long enough, and did sufficient mileage, you should have taught yourself how to run hills within training runs. It is now time to replace some of the hilly courses with hill repetitions.

Find a fairly steep hill, but a hill which you feel reasonably comfortable running up...three to four degrees, or a three percent grade works well for most runners. Steeper hills do give you faster rewards, but they place greater strain on the Achilles tendon and calf muscles. You'll need to use 100 to 1,200 meter hills for these sessions.

Reformed marathon runners may need to emphasize short hill reps to improve knee lift and legspeed. Recent 5K specialists may need longer reps up gentler inclines for speed endurance. All 5K and 10K runners will benefit from running both types of hill repeat.

When running hill repeats, you'll ignore some aspects of efficient form. Hill reps require a different action...an exaggerated running action which would be inefficient in a race, yet it's perfect for 5 and 10K strength training.

Lets assume you've decided to start with short reps. Use a 100 meter section to begin training.

Run one third of your planned mileage for this day as a warm-up; do your stretches. Then commence the first of say ten repetitions. But how?

Run up the hill with a high knee lift and sprinters type arm action.

The legs should not be going too fast...the emphasis is on lifting the knees higher than in normal runs...but landing softly.

Land closer to your toes than the heel of the foot...midfoot is ideal.

You will run more like a sprinter in these sessions than at any other time.

Pick a focal point close to the top of the hill; it helps prevent you from leaning forward.

Run perpendicular to the surface in hill repeats.

Walk back down the hill for recovery, and stride up it again.

For your next effort, try shorter, quick strides.

Run a variety of styles to practice knee lift, legspeed, full calf extension and arm movement. You will not look as pretty as when you're running hills in a race, but this practice will improve your strength, and from that added strength, your speed.

When you feel tired, or cannot fully recover in your rest period, stop. You can add more reps in future sessions. After the hill session, warmdown thoroughly to relax your muscles.

Hold back on the first session. 80-90 percent effort is all you need to develop your leg strength and cardiovascular endurance--avoid stressing your muscles too much. Lower leg tissues, the quadriceps and other hip flexors (which lift the thigh), the hamstrings, and your back may still be sore...gentle stretching should clear these aches.

The second time you do hills, try about eight repetitions of 200 meters. The third time, try five at up to 400 meters. Early on, keep the hill sessions 7-10 days apart; later, if you are a moderate to high mileage person, slip down to 4-5 days.

Don't Suffer.

Respect hill training. Increase the number of reps and steep'ness of the grade gradually. Take care of the Achilles'. Hills are not about suffering. The entire session should feel no harder than a ten mile run.

You should not take 2-3 days to recover from these sessions. Like after all speedwork, you should be able to complete a long run in comfort the day after a hill session. If you can't, you did too many hills, or you did them too fast for your current fitness level.

Be patient. You are stimulating an increase in the size of your muscle fibers and their ability to contract rapidly, and with short recoveries between each contraction. You are creating strength in your thigh, buttocks, and lower leg muscles: This strength and flexibility determines your stride length, which determines your speed.

If possible, finish some of the reps just over the top of the hill--you can then practice accelerating as the grade decreases. You can also practice this acceleration on your steady runs when you're feeling fresh...pick the pace up by ten seconds per mile for 20 strides, before settling back to your regular speed.

When you've become comfortable with hill repetitions, you can increase the quantity of reps and the speed. Always aim to run hills faster than in a race...using the unique running action described above.

But not when you move on to other speed training. Exaggerated arm movements powering you forward, and up the hill or sand-dune is fine for hill reps. But when you move on to Chapter Three to Five speedwork, keep the arms under control. Allow your arms to balance you as you let your legs propel you forward. Arm power is only good for short distances...think running style for the rest of your speed training.

Reasonable Hill Training Limit?
25 reps of the short hill section is about right;
10 or 12 of the long section may be its equivalent.
10 minutes of actual hill reps works best for most, or up to 5 percent of your weekly miles.

Meanwhile, add a rep or two until you're on the hill for thirty minutes--including the recovery sections.

When you get stronger you can run easy for the recovery. This reduces your rest period. Land softly while running back down the hill.

Alternatives: You can split the hill into sections. Stride up the first section of say 150 meters--run easy or walk up for thirty to sixty seconds--then stride the second section. You will have a longer recovery going back down to repeat the reps in pairs or triples. You might run six sets of two efforts in a session.

When you can handle a variety of hills in training, they will seldom be a problem in races. In a race or tempo run, always run them with economy...using a low knee lift and short but fairly rapid stride. Tuck in behind someone, get 'pulled' up the hill, then find the extra gear you've been practicing as you accelerate over the top.

Long Hill Repetitions.

Your short hill reps are likely to be at 5 kilometer race intensity because you've been advised to run with similar form to a sprinter. Long reps at 15K pace also give you excellent results. Anaerobic threshold pace is discussed at length in Chapter Three. You can get a jump on that Chapter, and gain huge endurance rewards, by running one hill session out of every four up a long gentle grade.

Half a mile to a mile, or 800 meters to 1,500 meters is a reasonable range. Work on, or think about the elements of form as you run up the 2-4 percent grade. Mud or other *harsh* surface is preferred. Don't be squeamish about adjusting your style as you negotiate sections with uneven footing--it's easier to adapt stride length to meet your needs at 15K pace than at 5K intensity.

Resistance must increase as you get fitter. The second or third time through this resistance training, find steeper hills, deeper mud or sand, or run longer reps such as 1,000s at the speed of your old 800s.

Hill Training Will:

Improve your racing speed by building strength in the quads, hamstrings, buttocks, calves and back.

Correct your form--you can't run hills well with bad form--those exaggerated arm movements are good for you.

Increase your anaerobic efficiency.

Strengthen your quads, resulting in fewer knee injuries. Hill reps cause few injuries...there is much less shock per stride.

Open your stride--despite running repetitions, fartlek, 200s, etc., a lot of distance training can decrease your stride length. Just remember to exaggerate the knee lift and the arm swing, while pushing off with your toes and calf muscles.

Enjoy the hill. Always enjoy the hill. Don't fight it...work with it.

Hills for Strength: From Running Dialogue.

Hills should be run properly with an exaggerated knee lift for the best effect.

Types of hill: short, medium and long. Seek a variety, otherwise you become brilliant at one hill, but rarely see your hill in a race.

Split the hill into sections for short recovery sessions.

* Use sand and mud hills for added resistance and heavy shoes.
* Accelerate over the top to practice race situation.
* Technique for hills in a race--relax, then accelerate.
Hills increase muscle elasticity and the range of motion at the foot and ankle--vital for faster running.

Alternative Resistance Training.

Moving through the airs resistance takes effort. Running just behind someone in a race can save you 25 seconds at ten kilometers.

Running into the wind can make a session of two hundred meter strides harder; you'll gain more fitness.

Run fartlek 200-600 meter efforts into the wind. Run an occasional stride with the wind for relaxation, while working on your form. Ask yourself: Are the knees up high enough to give a full stride? Are the calves and foot hugging the hamstrings and butt...to reduce the pendulum swing? Are you using your ankles and calves to the limit? Do your shoulders roll because you don't use the arms much? See the form hints on page 10.

See page 64 for mile repeats into the wind.

Grass, dirt trails, and beaches without slope, are perfect places to run. They're soft and uneven, forcing muscles and tendons to work harder than on a flat surface for the same speed. You become stronger by stressing your muscles. Gradually increasing the resistance is part of the overload principle--exercise to a modest degree of fatigue, but not to exhaustion. Rest to recover while the body adapts. You can then train harder next time.

More Resistance.

Run hills and other training on the softest surface you can find--it reduces the long term joint wear and tear; it reduces bone and muscle injuries. Running is about longevity, not a one event or race program, so run on soft surfaces for a lifetime of recreation.

Dirt, grass and sand, are better than concrete and asphalt. Seek out mud, snow and grass with a softened base. Top coaches recommend these soft surfaces which make you work harder for the same speed because:

The surface gives...you work harder at push-off.

You have to lift your feet higher to avoid tripping.

Wet or muddy shoes act like ankle weights.

Cross-country racing is discussed in Chapter Three.

Treadmill Running.

Use a fan to create your own breeze when treadmill running. Hang a fluid bottle on the side rail.

Don't cheat the machine by pushing yourself up instead of forward when treadmill running. There is no point in setting the treadmill well beyond your natural speed limit. Your running biomechanics will suffer.

Treadmill Hill Training drawbacks are the same as for all treadmill running! There are advantages though:

Fast running improves flexibility. Power yourself forward not upward with the calves to extend your stride. Decrease vertical bounce...the price of running half an inch too high can be 10 percent of your energy. Run forward to avoid this waste.

Treadmills allow you to set the grade accurately and to choose the hill length.

When you move house or State, you can run on the same hill for continuity.

No need to run downhill during the recovery--thereby reducing the pounding.

Your recovery can be close to the pace at which you were running up hill.

You can take shorter recoveries.

Sample Treadmill Session.

A possible treadmill hill session starts with a mile, or up to ten minutes warm-up. The running warm-up is short because most gym users will do 20 minutes of weights, and 10 minutes each at cycling and rowing, before commencing their favorite sport.

Begin the actual hill training with a quarter mile at 4 percent grade. The running speed could be 40 seconds per mile slower than ten kilometer pace...very easy when on the flat...but not when you have to raise the knees to account for the grade.

During the recovery quarter, run at the same speed--at least in theory--see below.

Often, we tend to jog in the recovery. The treadmill keeps you honest; you have to keep going. After a quarter rest at zero grade, repeat the 4 percent rep.

Then run two each at 5 and 6 percent. To complete a two mile session of hills, finish with a half mile...but at only 5 percent elevation. Then a pleasant warmdown, and this very time efficient training is over...at least for most people. If there is a treadmill time limit at your fitness club, the warmdown can be pool running. Most medium mileage runners should aim toward three miles of hill training in a workout.

One quirk of treadmill running is that the belt goes faster when you run uphill. At least on some machines. Perhaps it's because we are pushing off better with our toes, propelling the belt along, in addition to the motor's work. Whatever the reason, my machine gives me hill repeats at 6:40 mile pace, with the recovery at 7:00 pace. No complaints from me--it's better than the machine forcing me to do it the opposite way around.

If your machine allows you the same pace while recovering on the flat, you'll be running roughly marathon pace--the ideal pace for ridding muscles of their waste products from speedwork. Depending on your weight and race pace, you'll be at 15K to 5K intensity during treadmill hill reps, even if done at 40 seconds per mile slower than 10K speed.

It probably doesn't matter what grade of hill you use; the important thing is to run hill repeats. The speed is personal also--train at 15K and 5K intensity, plus two mile race pace effort if it suits you.

Maintain High Mileage.

You need to run mileage too of course. The long run and total mileage are unchanged during this phase. You will be getting fitter because a few of those miles are harder, more productive miles. Run at least eight sessions of hills in this build-up phase--then retain hills once every 10-14 days while training through Chapter Three and Four. Try once every 14 to 21 days in your racing phase.

Hill running builds the gastrocnemious muscle, the big calf muscle next to your skin. Try to include downhill running on even grass to develop the soleus muscle.

Downhill Running for Strength.

Yes...for strength. Strides and reps on soft 1-2 percent down-grades work hamstrings, gluteal muscles, hip flexors and the soleus--they make your running economic: Downhills will improve your biomechanics.

Downhills build strength in the hamstring muscles as they pull the lower leg rapidly through during the recovery phase, and strengthen the gluteal muscles as they extend the hip behind the runner.

Hip extensor muscles include the gluteus maximus muscle and gluteus minimus muscle. Taken together, they are called the gluteal muscles, the gluts, the butt muscles or the glutei muscles. Which makes looking them up on the Internet entertaining or frustrating depending the kind of day you're having.

The main hip flexor muscles are the iliosoas group (Iliacus muscle and Psoas major muscle), and the biceps femoris muscle (or quadricep femoris muscle), one part of the quadriceps muscle. They lift or flex the upper leg--they give us our knee-lift.

If you're warmed up and stretched, proceed to:

The best stride frequency is 90-95 per minute. Increasing from 90 to 92 per minute can shave 60 seconds from your 10K. Increase your cadence by practicing: Short, rapid strides for 30-60 seconds. Fast leg action with short up-hills. Swift strides and reps down a gentle hill.

Downhill Running to Improve Economy.

The slope should be gentle--one to two percent is sufficient.

The surface should be soft: Short grass, fairly even sand or dirt trails, or an old railroad bed, or:

Use a treadmill...if it has the ability.

The First Hill Session.

Just like you would any other form of training, start with gentle strides. The first few sessions must be easy ones to get your muscles used to the faster legspeed, and an extended stride.

When you're loose...push off with the calf muscles to go faster.

Make full use of the hip extensor muscles to extend the work of the calf muscles.

Be conscious of your leg pull-through; whip the leg forward with the hip flexor muscles.

Think leg speed as you tear down the slope.

Work your hamstring muscles to speed the leg through; bring the lower leg closer to your butt than you normally do.

Do not run so fast that your butt muscles hurt.

Land softly...midfoot, and roll, then push rapidly off the toes after the support phase.

Run Perpendicular to the Slope.

Leaning forward can strain the gluteal and hamstring muscles. Leaning back puts pressure on the back and hip flexors. You'll be setting up a breaking action. You want a flowing, rhythmic biomechanically sound running style.

Intermediate Downhill Running.
200-400 meter efforts. Short intervals.

Run modest numbers to begin with--about two thirds of your normal interval session--because you'll be running them faster. You will be close to mile race pace while putting in 2 mile pace effort.

Think about your running biomechanics. Sprinting downhill with arms flying all over the place will not make you a more economical runner.

Push the arms back on each stride, allow them to move straight forward to their natural height; don't grasp for handfuls of air. Hands don't need to go across the chest...unless it's the perfect running form for your body. Straight back and forward to a modest height is best. The arms need to balance the legs: Think RELAXATION.

Advanced Downhill Training.

After three or four sessions of short efforts, move on to:

Long Repetitions at VO2 max. 800 to 1,200 meter intervals at 2 mile pace.

Actually, you can run 2 mile pace at 5K effort.

Running at 2 mile pace will be easier than on the flat. Enjoy flight during your training. Your heart and lungs will be at 5K pace, but the hip flexors and extensors get the benefit from two mile pace. Run one out of four long rep sessions downhill, and your track reps at 5K pace will seem easier...because you will have the legspeed.

Long downhill reps helped Sebastian Coe to two Olympic 1,500 meter Golds, they can help you too.

Chapter 2: Hills and Resistance.

An additional bonus to downhill speedwork is the long rest. Unless you've been driven out to the top of a long grade, or run a four mile warm-up to the top, you have to run back up the hill after each rep. My personal preference is to run one gentle uphill stride at the midpoint of the return journey; it helps to keep me loose, and the muscles warm.

Downhill Running Uses:
Cruising a few strides is pleasant when you feel tired; you still get to run fast. However, don't substitute downhills for the rest which you may need.
Race preparation at all distances, because you can run faster than race pace.
Preparation for downhill race courses such as the Desert News 10K in Utah.
Improved flexibility.
And finally, you can work on running economy without being under as much physiological or lung busting pressure as when you're running on the flat.

"**Consistency Pays Off**," says two time US Masters Gold Medalist at 10,000 meters, Greg Horner. "Take the first step when you don't feel like going for a run."
Horner does these sessions routinely.
The long run--18-23 miles.
Up-Hill work. 800-1,600 meters, but with the last 25 percent of it down a gentle grass slope.
Long repeats. Miles at 5K to 10K pace.
Short repeats. 800s at 5K pace; 400s at 3 seconds faster than 5K pace--about 2 mile pace or 100 % VO2 Max.

Pool Running.

Water can save your muscles and joints. You can take your hip flexors and extensors through a huge range of motion, but you'll get no damage from an over-striding impact. Use water running wisely. Don't jump into a session the day before your main speedwork training run. Your hip flexors are likely to be tired after the first pool run, so save it for the day AFTER speed training.

Think about your arm motion. You can soon develop bad running form habits if you're doing high training volume in the wet stuff. Use a flotation device if it feels right for you.

You don't have to restrict your pool running to rest days. You can run a hard session at threshold pace or VO2 max pace in the pool also: The next day do your easy running on land.

Protect your Achilles and Calf.

The main stretches were shown on pages 22 to 25. Now we'll take a look at stretching the calf muscles properly--which helps the rest of the leg muscles fall into place, and keeps your running biomechanics sound. Use these stretches to decrease Achilles Tendinitis and calf muscle strains. An appropriate length calf muscle reduces the pressure and the potential strain on the Achilles. The muscle tendon unit, where the muscle joins the tendon, is the most likely place to strain. Work with your muscle tendon unit...not against it.

Slow muscle stretching, no bouncing, is the best way to avoid muscle strains. Your Golgi organs, called proprioceptors--determine the stretch reflex. Hold each stretch for 20-30 seconds until the muscle reflex unit relaxes, then ease down a bit more for the full muscle stretch. Work with the proprioceptors while stretching for increased muscle flexibility.

The Calf Muscle is Two Muscles.

The gastrocnemius' muscle origin, or the attachment to connective tissue closest to the heart, is above the knee--it is best stretched with a straight knee. The soleus' muscle origin is below the knee, and is best stretched with a bent knee.

A/ The lunge (as in a sword fight), is suitable for both muscles. The gastroc is stretched by keeping the heel of the back leg on the ground.

The front leg goes well forward--keep your balance and stay tall. In this upright position, lean forward until you feel the stretch in the straight back leg.

By placing the front foot flat on a chair, you can give the soleus an extra stretch. Push the bent knee forward with the hands until the muscle starts to feel a little tight.

B/ Stand with your toes on a step or stair with the heel flat and extended over the edge. Allow the heels to drop down slowly until resistance is felt in the muscle or tendon: hold for the usual time before pushing up (which is, of course, exercise). John Pagliano D.P.M. a recognized injury expert for Runner's World, suggests that, "People with high arches may want to give this exercise a miss because it can overstretch their Achilles complex." Do some with straight knees; do some with knees bent.

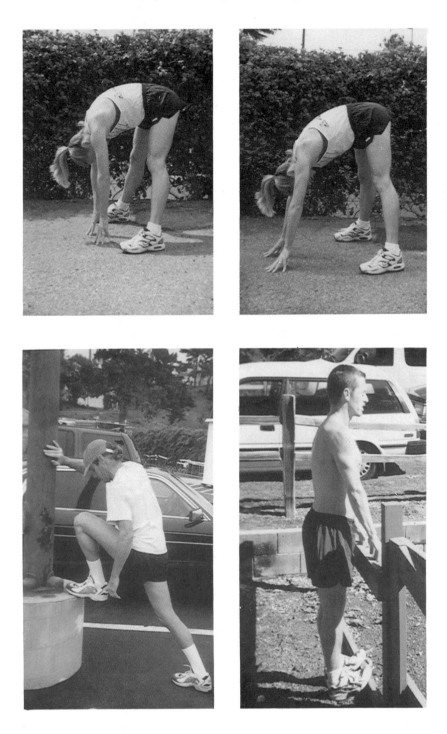

Chapter 2: Hills and Resistance.

The mis-named pushing the wall down. If you push, you're working the calf muscles--you should not work and stretch at the same time. With the step exercise you have two distinct phases...work and stretch. With this next stretch, simply lean in towards the support.

C/ To stretch the gastrocnemius muscle, stand 3-4 feet from a wall, and put your outstretched hands on the wall shoulder width apart. Keep the knee straight and the heels flat on the ground. Lean in toward the wall slowly, keeping the body and knee straight: Stop when you think the calf is at its limit...when it or the Achilles tendons feel stretched.

D/ For the soleus muscle:

--as above, but 2-3 feet away. Bend the knees until you feel the stretch--again, keep heels on the ground.

E/ Ropes, pulleys, etc.

Place a piece of rope under the sole of your foot, then pull it up to give your calf muscle a stretch. As always, use a bent knee for the soleus muscle and straight knee for the gastrocnemius muscle.

F/ Walking your fingers to your feet.

I like this one. Feet facing forward, place your hands on the floor in front of you...well in front of you. Straighten your legs--though locked knees are not essential. Now, walk your hands back toward your toes. Hold, relax per usual, then get a little closer to your toes as you improve flexibility.

The very flexible person will be able to do this stretch with palms on the floor. Those with less muscle flexibility can walk back on the fingers until the stretch is felt in the back of the legs. Whichever way you do it, keep your balance. Keeping your legs a foot or two apart may help you maintain balance. It also makes you feel better because your arms are closer to the ground...your muscles appear to be more flexible. How much weight you put on those running arms is your decision.

G/ At your desk or home, you can use one of the stretch gizmos on the market, or simply use a triangle of wood. Place your feet on the gismos at an appropriate angle to maintain or gain flexibility.

H/ Perhaps the simplest stretch. Any time you are standing round waiting, place one leg about six inches out in front of you. Keep most of your weight on the supporting leg; rest lightly on the heel of the leg to be stretched. Dorsi-flex the foot--use those cute little shin muscles to pull your toes up toward your shin. Hold for ten seconds and repeat. This exercise will also decrease your shin splint risk.

When doing most of your hamstring stretches, you can also stretch the calf muscles.

Hamstring muscle stretches with a straight leg are best--with a nearly locked knee. During your hamstring stretches, simply dorsi flex the foot, bring the toes toward your shin, and you have two stretches at one time. You'll maintain good calf flexibility while doing your hamstring stretches.

Preventing Achilles Tendon Injuries.

Shortening of the Achilles tendon and calf muscle is a big part of the problem. Avoid high heels...you don't have to follow the fashions.

Heel inserts are a great aid to reducing strain on the Achilles tendon. Inserts are not effective unless you also work on the flexibility aspect with whichever two or three of the above stretches you prefer. Heel insert use is to some degree an admission that you are unwilling or unable to stretch the calf muscles!

Overpronation and other factors damage the Achilles tendon: a FULLY stretched pair of calf muscles, gastrocnemius and soleus, is your first line of defense against damage to the tendon, to the muscles, and to that all important muscle tendon unit. Make stretching a regular habit, and you will maintain as much flexibility as your body design is capable of.

Injuries are often due to imbalances. In addition to stretching the calf, do strengthening exercise for the shin muscles--which in runners, are often weak.

Bounding.

When you reach your flexibility limits, you can add Bounding.

Bounding is a great strength session. Bring it in a few strides at a time.

When running on a soft surface or up a hill, bound forward with an exaggerated high knee-lift, and a fast running action. Bounce off the toes forcefully as you power your body up and forward--much higher and further than usual--then land softly. Do 20-30 meters at a time with a walk down or jog back recovery.

If you have wide stairs or steps available, do double leg jumps up them. Hopping is an effective variation on bounding, and allows you to isolate each leg. Hop or jump up a grassy slope, in sand, or through mud. Land softly.

Sand is the preferred surface for all these exercises because your legs struggle to propel you forward, and your arms work to maintain your balance--you get a whole body workout. You also get a soft landing. Stay tall and relaxed.

You'll develop your hip flexors, calves and quadriceps. These stronger muscles will increase your stride, speed, and decrease your risk of injury.

Include a few minutes of skipping rope for the calves, but limit these plyometrics. You want to build power to enhance your endurance--you get fast by being strong--yet you have to avoid the bulk of a sprinter.

Weight Training:

Include weight training wisely...do many reps, using modest amounts of weight--about 60 percent of the maximum which you can lift. The American College of Sports Medicine recommends:

At least eight separate exercises for different muscle groups.

Two or more sets of 8-12 reps for each exercise.

Lifting at least twice a week.

Free weights to bring your balancing muscles into play, but use good lifting technique.

Breathe in a normal way. Don't hold your breath. Machines allow you to isolate a particular muscle. Leg extensions, hamstring curls and the leg press cover your upper leg muscles. Do tricep and bicep curls for the arms, and sit-ups or crunches to help your posture.

According to John Brennand, US National Masters Gold Medalist on road, cross-country and track, and the 1998 60-64 age group 5,000 & 10,000 meter track Champion,

"Strengthening exercises are particularly important for masters runners.

"Stride frequency is the same, but stride length decreases with age after the mid forties.

"We run slower because we are not as strong.

"We run more efficiently if the body is stronger."

Brennand likes this exercise for the trunk.

Start by kneeling on the ground, resting your weight on forearms and knees. Raise your left arm and right leg to a horizontal position; hold them perpendicular to the floor for a count of five, and return to the starting position. Do two sets of 10 for each pair of appendages.

Brennand recommends this upper leg exercise.

Single Leg Drop.

Stand on one leg, on a bench or low chair about knee high. While standing upright, bend your supporting leg until you touch the ground with the toe of your resting leg. Without an assist from the restive leg, push your body back up. Keep the body upright as much as possible. Do three sets of 10. After a few weeks you can hold weights to add resistance.

In addition try...**Half Squats.**

Feet should be shoulder width apart for balance. Use hand weights early, a lightly weighted barbell when you have become skilled. A half inch heel boost may help you balance. Bend at the knees while keeping the back erect. Go down slowly to the level of comfort for your knees, about halfway for most runners; thighs will typically be parallel to the floor. Push up quite fast. Your muscles work on the way down, and on the way up!

Chapter 2: Hills and Resistance.

Traditional Leg Lunges.

Same position as above, but with your feet together. Take a step forward, drop down into the lunge, then push with the lead leg to regain your original position.

Old faithful Step-ups.

Using a bench, chair or a pair of steps about 18 inches high, step up with one leg. Straighten this lead leg to pull yourself up. Step back down slowly with the lead leg. Unless you want to work them, don't push off with the calf muscles. Change lead leg half way through the reps.

These four exercises work the quadriceps, hamstrings and gluteals--the power muscles for running; plus the back, abdominal and side muscles while you work at keeping your balance.

Here's Brennand's favorite lower leg exercise .

Stand on a low step or staircase with the right foot on the higher level, and your weight on the left forefoot at the lower level. Using the right foot for balance, bounce rapidly ten times on the left foot. Do three sets of ten for each foot.

Or do...**Heel Raises**.

Stand on the balls of your feet on a two inch block or a stair. Raise your heels up, then roll up onto your toes. Drop gently back down so that the heel dips below the step. Keep a steady and rhythmic movement.

Alphabet or numbers and Shin Lift.

While sitting in a chair, raise your feet and write the alphabet or zero to nine several times with your toes.

In a similar position, or sitting on a table, use a weight round your foot. Move the foot up and down from the ankle. This is often called the paint-pot exercise.

These four exercises work the gastrocnemius and soleus in the calf, which extend the foot, giving you your power at stride-off; and the tibialis anterior (the major shin muscle).

"It takes months of regular weights and resistance training before you see results," says Brennand, "Do make it a regular part of your training."

Add a couple of bicycle rides to this strength training...and oxen will be jealous of your power. Develop the strength which helps you to maintain form and speed despite your race fatigue. Leaning forward (when tired) can lead to muscle strains at the back of the legs--the hamstrings and glutei's or gluteals.

Ten to twelve weeks at this strength phase should allow you to rest three times for a race. One race each at 5K, 10K and 10 miles would be excellent experience for the fairly new runner, for the person coming down from the marathon, and would be perfect for the experienced runner too. Don't rest up very much though. Your major peak should be in 16 to 26 weeks. The races here are for training and for personal delight--and perhaps for bragging rights if the distance is new to you. Then it will be time to take your leg strength into the next phase.

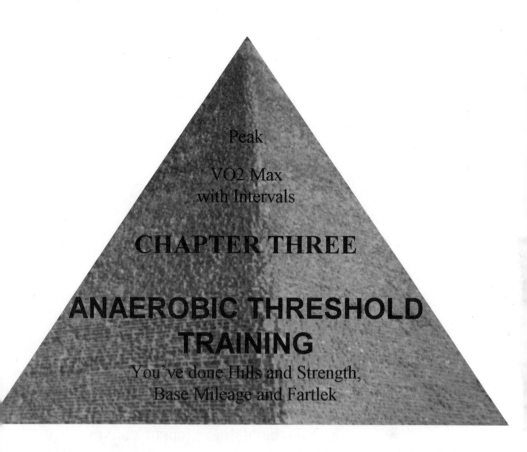

Peak

VO2 Max
with Intervals

CHAPTER THREE

ANAEROBIC THRESHOLD TRAINING

You've done Hills and Strength,
Base Mileage and Fartlek

Tempo running, or anaerobic threshold pace training is the author's third element in 10K and 5K preparation. Many runners will prefer to do this section before hill training. The order is not important; running each type of training is vital.

Threshold pace training involves Tempo Running or Cruise Intervals at 15K or 10 mile race pace--about 10-20 seconds per mile slower than 10K speed. Running slower than 10K and 5K speed will actually improve your ability to run a great 5 or 10 kilometer race.

Sounds far-fetched doesn't it! Yet slowish running at 65-70 percent of maximum heartrate improved your aerobic ability, your VO2 max, when you ran a minute to one and a half minutes per mile slower than 10K pace.

Likewise, running about 15 seconds slower than 10K pace will improve your anaerobic threshold, the point at which you produce ever increasing amounts of lactic acid. According to Jack Daniels Ph.D., researcher, coach of the over achieving State University of New York at Cortland cross-country team, and author, "Anaerobic Threshold is the pace or intensity beyond which blood lactate concentration increases dramatically, due to your body's inability to supply all its oxygen needs."

Process More Oxygen

"Physiologically, threshold training teaches muscle cells to use more oxygen--you produce less lactate. Your body also becomes better at clearing lactate."

Threshold pace running conditions your muscle fibers to a faster pace. You build leg strength and improve running biomechanics by testing the limits of your aerobic system.

Because you're running at a fast pace for considerable distance, you develop speed endurance by bringing in more of your fast twitch muscle fibers.

As coach Roy Benson says, you teach "motor responses to more of the muscles...used in racing."

At threshold pace, the mitochondria in your muscle cells can no longer meet all of your energy needs. Your body switches to the anaerobic system--you produce energy in the fluid surrounding the mitochondria. You produce lactic acid as a by-product to anaerobic threshold running. Practice running at this pace often enough and you will adapt to running with a higher level of lactic acid in your muscle cells and circulatory system. You will also excrete more lactic acid.

The point at which you produce excess lactic acid is your red line. If you run faster than red line pace, your body will soon ask, then force you to slow down. In the early stages of threshold training your red line will probably be 80 percent of max HR. According to Daniels, "As you get fitter, your red line rises from 80 percent of maximum heartrate to 90-95 percent. Race day red line speed rises."

In fact, had you attempted threshold pace running before a base mileage and fartlek build-up, your red line would have been closer to 70 percent max HR.

How do you start your Anaerobic Threshold or Lactate Buffering or Lactate Capacity enhancing Intervals and Tempo Runs?

You already have.

The 10K and 5K races which you did in the past few months were well over your red line, but they still helped to raise your threshold limit. However, 15K pace is easier to maintain in training, and just as effective at raising your anaerobic threshold, so let's back off on the 10K speed by 15 seconds per mile.

Give your body time to adjust to the new demands you're placing on it. Run half marathon pace first. Then, apply the *least* amount of pressure or training needed to raise your anaerobic threshold. 15K pace is best. You'll find the correct speed instinctively...if you practice.

After a good build-up of base work at 60-80 percent maximum heartrate, strides, fartlek and hill reps plus other strength training, you can do your first real session at threshold pace.

Mile reps at 80-85 percent max HR--cruised in control--is a very relaxing way to get used to threshold pace running. Two of these sessions will prepare you for your Tempo runs. Run up to 10 percent of your weekly mileage as a session of long reps at 20-30 seconds slower than 10K race pace--about half marathon pace.

Half marathon pace is Lactate Threshold Velocity, the highest speed you can run without the build-up of lactic acid. You need to experience some lactate build-up, so after a few sessions you'll increase speed to 15K pace.

How Hard is Threshold Pace?

This threshold pace training should feel comfortably hard--not excruciatingly hard. Your goal is to get fitter. You will not improve your fitness if you avoid these sessions due to fear of hurting while you run. Running too fast will also make you prone to injury (though the biggest injury predictors are high mileage and sudden changes in training). It takes regular runs at threshold pace to obtain the huge gains in speed endurance which this type of training provides.

How huge? Most 10K runners think a one minute improvement on their personal record is huge. The first time through this phase can give you that 10 seconds per mile race pace increase. Those of you who have been racing for years should expect less--unless you've never done regular training at 15K pace.

Increasing your pace too often will increase injury potential; don't increase pace more than once every three weeks. Instead, try to relax while running at the same speed...with less effort. Maintain the same effort level in hot, cold or windy conditions, and on hilly courses. Don't worry about the pace changing. Heartrate and how you feel at this effort level are the best indicators.

Next up:

Continuous runs at threshold pace.

Run about 6 miles at half marathon race pace--probably 80 percent of your max heartrate. Six miles is simply the goal of course, or 10 percent of your weekly mileage--whichever is the least amount.

Early threshold sessions should be barely over 80 percent max heartrate--though you've been running quality stuff before, you need to get used to the effort involved during a continuous fast run. You'll also need to think about form on these runs. Comfortably hard is not all-out running. Build from five percent of your monthly miles to 10 percent. Run a threshold pace session every 5 days or so; keep them short enough that you can maintain your other quality sessions which complement threshold pace.

Graduate to 15K Pace.

After about three to five runs at half marathon pace, you can try 4 miles at 15K or 10 mile pace...which is true threshold tempo speed--taking you to 85-86 max HR. Hopefully you won't accumulate much lactic acid because your body is learning how to break it down.

Then move to one and a half mile or two mile repeats at 90 percent max HR--but only if it feels right, you must not feel too uncomfortable. Restrain yourself to 10 percent of your training miles at these paces.

After a few weeks, you'll be able to increase pace on your continuous 4 mile runs towards 90 percent maximum heartrate. Many physiologists recommend 90 percent max HR as the top range for these sessions. Most of these runs will be at 15K or 10 mile pace to hit that pulse target. When your muscles are tired two days after your long run, or when weather is bad, it may only be half marathon pace: It will rarely be slower. If your heartrate is over 90 percent at your half marathon pace, you should add rest to the next few days. Don't be concerned if you're able to run 10K pace at 90 percent max. These good days are a joy...provided you're not overtraining. Aching quads is one sign of overtraining...back off on pace to 15K speed.

Faster than 10K pace puts most of us over the red line--it is too harsh. As Jack Daniels says, "86 percent of maximum heartrate is probably the best pace." Which is about 10 seconds per mile slower than 10K pace if you've never raced at 15K or 10 miles.

Once you've run 10 sessions working on your Lactate Buffering Capacity, alternate sessions of continuous Tempo running with the Cruise Intervals.

You'll decrease rep times rapidly at first as you become more economical for 5-10 minutes at 15K pace. Extra improvement is slower. It occurs when your threshold has changed; when you produce less lactic acid.

High Mileage Runners:

Six to eight miles of long reps at anaerobic threshold or faster is a popular session for high mileage people. Many Kenyans do eight times one mile at 10K pace or faster on dirt trails; the next week it could be 10 to 12 times 1,000 meters at 5K pace, with a 400 meter or a one minute rest at marathon pace--the ideal "restive" pace for muscles to deal with lactic acid.

Mere Mortals!

Don't do more than 10 percent of your mileage in one speed session, but try this four week rotation if you race once a month.

At fifty miles a week, you're entitled to five miles of threshold pace reps.

4 x 2,000 meters at 15K pace equals your true threshold pace. Take a quarter mile slow run recovery.

5 x one mile at 10K pace. Faster than threshold for most runners, but it will help your buffering system. Avoid this pace if you've recently hit 50 miles per week for the first time.

8 x 1,000 at 15K pace...slower and shorter than last week, so keep the recovery to under one minute.

Resting up with...8 x 800 at 10K pace...but with a shorter rest than for the mile repeats.

You need to train up to the point at which anaerobic energy production predominates. Try to avoid going over the red line. Avoid running too fast--you don't make greater gains on your constantly changing anaerobic threshold speed by running at the faster pace. Generally,

15K is better than 10K pace; those of you on low mileage, or concentrating on the 5K, may feel the need to run some reps at 10K pace for psychological reasons. 15K pace makes you less tired, though, allowing a more worthwhile hill or VO2 max session later in the week.

Don't repeat training sessions more than once every three weeks. If you elect to run them all at 15K pace, the 1,000s and 800s will need a 200 meter rest to make sure you give the muscles a chance to educate themselves--muscles need only a *short* chance to buffer and excrete the lactate. Long rests defeat your purpose.

Remember to match each threshold session with some kind of speed at short distances.

And don't forget your hills or resistance training.

Long Runs--Maintain Mileage.

Long distance runs remain unchanged during this phase--up to 15 miles, or one third of your average weekly mileage--at 65 to 70 percent max HR.

You should probably run a quality speed session the day before each long run--after all, you don't need fresh legs to run easy. After appropriate rest, you're ready for the second speed session of the week.

You should bounce back from speed sessions rapidly--if you cannot, then they are too hard for your current fitness level.

Be a Heretic.

Many coaches say you should decrease mileage by 10 percent while running speedwork, especially if you've done most of your running at one pace. They say your legs will be "dead and lifeless" from too much pounding. They'll be unable to develop much in terms of pace.

I disagree.

The leg strength will enable you to develop speed--from good stride length and from high cadence. Don't reduce your mileage, or you will lose that strength. Adapt to the faster pace. Run half marathon pace before 15K pace. Include fartlek and hills. There's no excuse for running at the same pace day after day.

This book takes exception to the sessions suggested for low mileage runners...because it contains the same percentage speedwork as high mileage runners. There's no reason to deny yourself an anaerobic threshold or VO2 max session simply because you run low mileage. You will benefit even more than high mileage runners.

Here is how you can combine resistance training with threshold pace to extend or finish the strength phase:

Cross-country Racing.

Not all of us have access to cross-country racing, but most of us can train as if we are running cross-country.

The British run a series of 4-6 mile races in the fall, then county and regional meets at 7-8 miles, followed by nationals at 9 miles. All clubs can take nine runners to the nationals; you don't have to be a sub 35 minute 10K, let alone sub 15 minute 5K person to make your team.

All of us can have a similar cross-country experience. Just find dirt, grass and mud sections which give a mile or more of running...over undulating surfaces if possible.

Week one...run 4 x one mile
Week two...2 x two miles
Week three...5 x one mile
Week four...2 x three miles
Week five...five miles hard
Week six...5 x one mile
Week seven...resting with 2 x two miles
Week eight...8 mile time trial

The time trial can include low stress U-turns. If your loop or section is one mile, simply stop the watch at the end, jog 15 meters while slowing to do a U-turn, then accelerate and re-start the watch for your return. These 15 seconds will give you a mental breather. At the end of your mile or two mile reps, however, take the one to two minute break recommended for threshold training.

You can use wind as a training tool.
Run mile repeats into the wind and your cardiovascular system will get a threshold pace workout while your leg muscles amble along at slower than half marathon pace. Achieve similar results by running up long gentle slopes.

If you want more legspeed, run reps with the wind or down gentle slopes. But go easy with those legs; don't enter phase four yet.

In overstriding, the foot is still traveling forward as it strikes the ground. The heel acts as a break, causing stress and damage on every stride. The damage could show itself as sore knees, aching soles of the feet, a tender back, or anything in-between. You will also lose momentum on every stride; you'll fatigue earlier.

Whether you run on trails, grass, road or the track, Anaerobic Threshold Training Builds Stamina.

Stamina is improved because you have:

Further increased your VO2 max.

Expanded your capillary network.

Increased your muscles' enzyme activity.

Educated your cells to tolerate high levels of lactic acid.

Educated your cells to excrete lactic acid more rapidly.

Threshold Training Improves Running Form.

Concentration on form improves--resulting in:

Increased running efficiency as you decrease wasted efforts.

Devouring more ground with each stride as your hip flexibility improves.

Further strengthening of your running muscles; you bring in more of your muscle fibers to maintain this fast pace.

Improved coordination at higher speeds...if you pay attention to form: you can't just float.

Threshold pace prepares you for the stresses of racing.

See the detailed schedules later, but this is how most people's training will look during Phase Three.

The 36-44 miles per week at high intensity.

Day one...13 miles

Day two & six...rest or an easy 4 miles

Day three...two miles of hill repeats (5 percent of mileage)

Day four...easy 4-6 miles

Day five...3-4 miles of fartlek

Day seven...4 miles of threshold running (10 percent of mileage). Alternate 4 x one mile; 2 x two miles; with a straight 4 miler. Pace guidelines on page 70--ease down from half marathon to 15K pace over 6-9 weeks.

You can use the miles from days 2, 4, and 6, to run two 6 milers, it will give you more endurance than the shorter runs.

The three quality sessions need a warm-up and cooldown of one to two miles.

The serious runner who is going through this system for the first time, or reaching 40 miles for the first time, will only do one or two quality runs per week. More schedule details for all levels on pages 140-149.

You may find threshold pace is the most enjoyable form of 10K and 5K training. You're running only a bit slower than 10K pace so you experience the exhilaration from near full-speed cruising. You're only running 3-4 miles at this lesser pace, so it certainly should not be exhausting. Your muscles should have a tingling freshness and buoyancy after you've showered. You should feel so good that you think about going straight out to repeat the session--but you must not. You'll limit yourself to one run every 4-5 days at threshold pace.

One Extra Mile at Speed.

When you've worked through this entire training system once, or you've done at least 10 threshold pace sessions, plus a few interval sessions from Chapter Four, you can add a little speed to your anaerobic training day.

Chapter 3: Anaerobic Threshold.

Simulate your race day situation by practicing running fast with tired muscles.

After a tempo run, do five quite fast, but not flat out, three to four hundred meter efforts--take a one to two hundred meter recovery. Despite the fatigue from the threshold part of your run, these reps can be quite fast.

Restrict yourself to 5K pace early on; after a few sessions, speed up to two mile pace. Your legs should still feel great. You should not be placing yourself, or your muscles, under great strain. Then, just like after all your threshold runs, warmdown with a mile or two of easy running.

The first two chapters concluded with stretching advice. So will Chapter Three. When you move onto VO2 max training in the next chapter, you will run a distinct warm-up, then do your stretches and strides, followed by the speedwork. Anaerobic threshold pace is so easy to attain that many runners neglect to stretch.

Injuries delay peak performances because you take long periods away from your sport. When coming back from injury it may only take a few weeks to regain most of your aerobic fitness and the ability to run well at threshold pace or modest speeds: It takes months to regain your full strength and the ability to run fast.

During threshold pace training, many runners cruise through a warm-up, then pick up the pace. This is time efficient. It's almost obligatory on hot or cold days, but do try at least one stretch. Stretching is best done with warm muscles, so find some shade on a hot day, or a wind sheltered spot on a cold day, and do this one all encompassing stretch.

The adapted lunge.

Place one foot on a support which is 18-24 inches high. Adopt the lunge position, keeping the heel of the rear foot on the ground. Lean into the supported leg to stretch the buttock muscles, while experiencing a gentle pull on the Achilles tendon and soleus muscle. You'll also feel a pull on the quadricep group of the supported leg. You should feel a gentle stretch on all posterior muscles of the rear leg, and on that Achilles. Arch your back to relax those muscles too. Repeat with the opposite foot on the support.

Buffering capacity, anaerobic threshold, lactate gigididoo...doesn't matter what we call it--the science backs it up. Cruising at 15K or 10 mile race pace brings huge rewards provided it is not over used. Six to ten sessions bring you most of your gains. Then run a few races and maintain the gains while working on the final aspect of your 10K and 5K running in Chapter Four.

How to use the Speed Table on page 70.

Your best recent 10K is the starting point. Your base threshold training pace is 15K speed, or 10-15 seconds per mile slower than 10K speed.

Though anaerobic threshold is best improved with the 15K pace sessions, low mileage runners may benefit from fewer reps at their 10K pace.

Lactate Threshold Velocity incorporates elements of threshold and VO2 max and running economy. It's the highest rate of using oxygen without the build-up of lactic acid. It also equals *half marathon* pace. Use this pace as preparation for 15K pace sessions, or while resting up. Two to three mile reps work well at this pace.

Use a mixture of sessions to meet your needs and the freshness of your legs on a particular day.

The mile personal record (PR) line shows you if you've done sufficient strength and mileage training. If the 5 minute miler cannot run 35.27 for 10K, he or she should add more steady runs, long runs, hills, fartlek and threshold, before moving to Chapter Four.

Try to make consecutive reps faster. Gain a sense of relaxation at speed. Push back your anaerobic threshold.

Anaerobic Threshold paces at 10K, 15K and half marathon speeds

PR at Mile	PR at 10K 6.21m	Mile Reps 10K Pace	Best 15K time	mile reps	for half marathon
4:20	**30:54**	4:59	48:19	5:11	pace,
4:30	**32:02**	5:10	50:02	5:22	add 12
4:40	**33:10**	5:20	51:34	5:32	to 15
4:50	**34:20**	5:32	53:27	5:44	seconds
5:00	**35:27**	5:43	55:09	5:55	per mile
5:10	**36:37**	5:54	56:51	6:06	
5:20	**37:50**	6:06	58:44	6:18	
5:30	**39:00**	6:17	60:26	6:29	from here
5:40	**40:09**	6:28	62:09	6:40	down, add
5:50	**41:15**	6:39	63:51	6:51	20 secs
6:00	**42:23**	6:49	65:24	7:01	
6:10	**43:29**	7:01	67:34	7:15	
6:20	**44:40**	7:12	69:17	7:26	
6:30	**45:56**	7:24	71:09	7:38	
6:45	**47:35**	7:40	73:38	7:54	from here
7:00	**49:18**	7:56	76:07	8:10	25 to
7:15	**50:41**	8:10	78:56	8:26	30 secs
7:30	**52:44**	8:30	81:43	8:46	
7:45	**54:41**	8:48	84:30	9:04	
8:00	**56:26**	9:05	86:50	9:19	40-45
8:30	**60:06**	9:41	93:12	10:00	secs
9:00	**62:42**	10:08	97:33	10:28	
10:00	**69:16**	11:09	107:12	11:30	

The
Peak
is soon
You've done
Anaerobic Threshold,
Hills and Strength,
Base Mileage & Fartlek

CHAPTER FOUR

INTERVAL TRAINING at your VO2 MAXIMUM PACE

Runners with a high VO2 maximum absorb more oxygen; they can race faster.

Economic runners burn less oxygen at a given pace: they're frugal with oxygen use. They too can race faster.

The best 5K and 10K performances are run by athletes with high VO2 max and good running economy.

Regular training at 2 mile & 5K race pace improves both VO2 max and running economy.

The aims of Interval Training then, are:

Improve Maximum Oxygen Uptake Capacity or VO2 Max--the amount of oxygen which you absorb.

Get more efficient at utilizing the oxygen you absorbed.

Improve leg turnover and running economy.

The easy running in Chapter One did not develop your neurological pathways for fast running, or use all the muscle fibers needed for fast running: which is why you ran fartlek during that phase of your training. The fartlek element did train the fast twitch muscle fibers, preparing those fibers for VO2 max training. The emphasis of Phase Two was to make those muscle fibers stronger; Phase Three was for speed endurance. Phase Four will take your running speed to a much higher level, while improving your running economy. You can run your hills and threshold pace after this phase if you wish--I will not deduct seconds from your personal records if you follow a different order.

Just what does VO2 MAX mean?

VO2 max, or Maximum Oxygen Uptake Capacity, to use its formal name, is the amount of oxygen we can absorb into our cells in one minute while working at full capacity. It's a measure of fitness expressed in milliliters per kilogram per minute.

You can predict your VO2 max with 95 percent accuracy by running around a track on a windless day for 15 minutes. The distance run to the nearest 25 meters is noted, and Bruno Balke's formula is used to predict VO2 max. After a base of 6.5, this follows a linear pattern of 5 mls/min/kg. for every extra 400 meters covered. For example, if you run 10 laps (4,000 meters), it predicts 56.5 mls/min/kg. 4,400 meters gives a 61.5 VO2 max. If 4,450 meters is run, VO2 max would be:

VO2 Max = 6.5 + 0.0125 x (distance run in 15 minutes)
        = 6.5 + 0.0125 x 4,450
VO2 Max = 62.125
World class runners have a figure of 80 (male) and 70 (female).

Frank Horwill, the BAF coach (The British Athletic Federation) quoted in Chapter One, whose system of training was used by Seb Coe, and many 28 minute 10K runners, says, "The best way to improve VO2 max is to run between 80 and 100 percent of VO2 max. One hundred percent equals the athlete's 3K pace; 95 % equals 5K speed; 90 % is 10K speed.

"Work physiologists believe training at 95 % VO2 max brings the best results--though one Russian physiologist of note--Karibosk, thinks 100 % (3K or two mile pace) is better because it tunes up the anaerobic pathway. Note--3,000 meters is run at 60 % aerobic and 40 % anaerobic.

"Physiologists are agreed the percentages at the higher level (100 -- 95 %) should be done for 3-5 minutes' duration, repeated many times in one session, with a short recovery. The lower percentages (90 -- 80 %) should be for 10-20 minutes, also with short recoveries."

Already worked through Chapter Three? You've trained at 80-90 percent VO2 max while running threshold pace sessions. This chapter deals with 90-100 percent VO2 max running.

At 2 mile pace, the heart, lungs and entire circulatory system work at maximum capacity to maintain speed. This stimulates your VO2 maximum to increase.

Months of long runs have increased your VO2 max substantially. Now it's time to make additional VO2 max gains by training at close to your maximum oxygen uptake pace. Applying this modest stress to your lungs, muscles and circulatory systems will stimulate your VO2 max to rise: you'll be able to race faster.

The Track.

You can run these sessions on a track--tracks create a more reliable yardstick to assess progress. Interval training is a precise and progressive form of training. You change one of Waldemar Gerschlers' 5 variables such as increasing pace by one second per quarter mile, once a month to:

further stimulate your VO2 system;

force you to run more economically;

use all your muscle fibers--making you stronger; and,

develop pace judgment.

These goals are best achieved on a flat surface of known distance.

The advantages to track sessions are:

1/ Same distances all over the country...within a couple of yards or meters.

2/ A smooth surface.

3/ You get away from traffic, dogs and pedestrians.

There are some track rules. Look before you change lanes; avoid lane one if possible; and if you think someone ahead of you is going to veer left to the inside after his interval, chances are, he will actually veer right. Assume everyone else's brain is malfunctioning, and you should stay safe. Don't expect to educate all the joggers and walkers. If you can persuade a few to stay out of the inside two lanes, you've achieved more than most runners have experienced. Most are beyond our help.

Rest During Interval Training.

The rest period is the Interval! Generally, you should take less than 90 seconds rest during interval sessions. The greatest stimulation of heart development occurs in the first 10 seconds of the rest period. If you're running reps at the appropriate pace for you, it should only take 30 seconds for the heartrate to get below 130. The extra minute is for your mind, not your body. There is no need to wait for your H.R. to reach 90. Let it reach 110-120 while maintaining a decent recovery speed. Running at a respectable jog during your recoveries brings in nutrients and helps the muscles to get rid of the accumulated wastes.

Strong enough for Interval Training?

You need a good base before commencing serious speedwork. Never lose sight of the strength phase. Keep your long runs and the modest pace threshold sessions throughout the year.

Your mileage and strength base increased the number and size of your mitochondria, the organelles inside the muscle cells that make ATP (adenosine triphosphate), which fuels your muscles. The strength you gained in Chapter Two and Three will allow you to run this sub 10K pace training--and often sub 5,000 pace running. Your patient strength build-up facilitates your shift to speedwork.

Interval Training Basics.

Do a warm-up and stretch. Flexibility determines your range of movement, your potential stride length. Muscles are 10 percent longer when warmed up. Muscles work better when they are long--exerting the same amount of force but with less effort.

Don't jump straight into long sessions of intervals.

Feel as comfortable in the last 400 meters as you did in the first 400.

Run the last few reps as fast as the early ones.

But don't make the last few significantly faster.

Don't feel wasted afterwards. Feel as if you could have run another 200 meters at that pace at the end of each rep; feel as if you could have run several more reps when you've completed the session.

Whether training on your own, or in a group, here's how you can progress if doing formal VO2 max training for the first time. See page 90 for the table of suggested training speeds at 95 and 100 percent of VO2 max.

* Week one--Bends & straights--stride along the straight and jog the bends at a steady pace. Run eight to twelve laps--giving sixteen to twenty-four striders--you should not feel exhausted. Short striders of 20-30 seconds require little concentration.

* Week two--16 x 200 meters with 200 interval recovery. The surface may tempt you to run faster; hold back to decrease injury potential.

* Week three--10 x 300 meters. A little slower speed than the 200s; take a 300 recovery. Run two straights and one bend for the repetition; two bends and a straight

for the recovery. Use lane 4 or 5. This reduces the strain on your ankles, knees and hips--there is a tendency to lean into the curves.

* Week four--8 x 200 and 4 x 400 meters. You will need to run a little slower than your 300 pace in order to keep going for the extra 100 meters.

Pace should be no faster than 2 mile race speed...100 percent of VO2 maximum, or about 10 seconds per mile faster than your best recent 5,000 meters. Sessions at this modest pace give your leg muscles a chance at adjusting to the track surface.

Use the sprinters start point when running in the middle lanes. The relay boxes are also a useful guide. Otherwise, running in lane five adds 26.8 meters per lap if the lanes are 42 inches wide. That's about 5.4 seconds for the 80 seconds per 400 meter runner.

* Week five--10 x 300 again. Pace judgment will improve with practice; aim to run them fairly even. If you run more than 40 miles per week, build toward at least fifteen reps.

* Week six--4 x 200 and 6 x 400 meters with the same jog recovery. Even with a full lap recovery, this session is quite hard. Aim to maintain good form for the entire lap...assess yourself in each hundred. Ask...is my form going? Quarters have the advantage that you start and finish each effort at almost the same place.

* Week seven--4 x 300, and 3-4 x 600.
* Week eight--6 x 200, and 3 x 800 meters.

Then alternate sessions using mostly short reps at 2 mile pace, with sessions of longer reps at 5K race pace. See the sample sessions in the schedule chapters.

This speedwork helps you get the greatest possible amount of the energy from your highly trained running muscles. Use the form hints from Chapter One, such as:

Don't run high. Half an inch too high can cost you 10 percent of your energy. Short, fast strides are often better.

Keep your hips forward.

Think about the elements of good form. It helps you to maintain efficient form for longer periods.

As the months and years progress, you'll become less bouncy, and more efficient at running...if you practice.

Track Psych-out?

You don't have to run these sessions on a track. You can use a watch with a beeper to run a session of one or two minute efforts with a minute rest...on grass, or paths and road. A mixture of track and hill sessions or fartlek will give you two sessions of short efforts a week. Do retain a tempo run or a session of long reps each week.

Tracks can help you keep interval training precise in any city; you can measure your progress, and the eventual decline as you age.

Intervals fine-tune your body; they help you get the best out of yourself. Measure the real progress in racing though. Don't just become good at interval sessions.

Practice good form, and intervals at close to VO2 max will:

Improve your flexibility and running efficiency...enabling you to race faster.

Recruit even more of your fast twitch fibers, more of your total fibers to shift your limbs at this pace. Which:

Improves your leg strength and therefore your stride length--allowing you to run faster.

Raises your leg turnover or cadence.

Improves overall speed and economy.

Your smoother running requires less ATP--your energy lasts longer. You can run farther at a set pace.

Your pace judgment improves.

You improve your neuromuscular coordination even if you forget to work on form.

You breathe deeper--intercostals and diaphragm muscles develop tone.

Your anaerobic buffering system is enhanced; your lactate tolerance goes up. Which means that your muscle fibers will contract despite the presence of high levels of lactic acid.

The body's ability to process oxygen improves.

Your aerobic capacity and VO2 maximum rises.

You're able to run longer before you reach oxygen debt...and you'll be better able to handle that debt...at a given speed.

You race faster.

You can even talk during the rest interval. The running becomes social.

VO2 Max Intervals are Progressive.

You apply a load--your body adapts--you're better able to handle that load a few weeks later...provided you include sufficient rest. Intervals are precise--you can measure your progress.

You can run at the pace of race distances you've no desire to race, and it will improve your race times. You may never race at two miles, but reps at this pace will help your 10K and 5K times.

You make huge early gains...provided you have enough background endurance.

This economical or controlled running is great preparation for races.

It's easier to concentrate on fast running when you race.

You can train at 90, 95 and 100 percent max heart rate with minimal risk of injury...to your mind or your body.

You can run 10K of reps at 10K pace...and it will feel easier than a race. Yet the next day, you won't feel as if you did a 10K race. Of course you will feel as if you trained very hard, perhaps as if you'd raced four miles. With good base, you can do an intense workout, yet you won't feel as if you've punished yourself.

Once you've learnt how to do them, one session a week of intervals can be done anywhere.

Just make sure you do short and long rep interval sessions at all race paces. For example, do 400s AND miles at 5K pace; do 300s AND 1,000s at two mile pace.

Have a Naturally High VO2 Max?

Runners with superb speed, a natural ability to run at 800 or mile race pace, should probably work on their endurance to maintain the fast pace longer--do more anaerobic threshold and steady runs to improve base endurance. But run plenty of VO2 intervals to work on your form.

Those who feel super relaxed at 15K pace, yet lack speed, should do strength and speedwork to develop their two mile race potential to their limit. Increasing VO2 max will benefit them at the 5K and 10K.

However, train at your weak area in moderation while continuing to practice your strengths. Adhere to the general rule of alternating 15K pace with 2 mile pace speedwork, and you won't go far wrong.

To Progress with VO2 Max Training.

John Babington, 1996 US Olympic Women's distance coach; coach to three times World Cross Country champion and Olympic Bronze Medalist at 10,000 meters, Lynn Jennings, and a regular contributor to Runner's World, says:

"There's no single correct formula for interval training. Training benefits can be achieved over a wide range of paces. An Interval workout is a function of several variables:

Pace;

length of runs;

recovery time...and

total workout volume

can all be adjusted in a variety of ways to produce sessions that are challenging and stimulating."

As Horwill suggests, the best results are obtained between 5K and 2 mile race pace.

To make progress then...the speed, or number of efforts at 200, 300 or 400 which you run at a given speed need to increase over a period of years--improving your VO2 maximum capacity and your running economy.

You can:

* Run faster in the effort--two mile race pace instead 5K pace--100 percent VO2 max instead of 95 percent.

* Take a shorter distance recovery--as your body adapts to fast running, your heartrate will recover to 120 beats per minute faster. You may only need a fast 200 jog instead of 400.

* Put more effort into the recovery (running at marathon pace for a minute instead of walking).

* Increase the number of efforts...slowly...towards 10K of speedwork, or 10 percent of your weekly mileage.

The prudent runner will only change one of the above factors at a time. If you're intending to run mainly 5,000 meter races, you should increase the speed of intervals until running faster than 5K race pace...2 mile pace is ideal--then steadily decrease the recovery period session by session.

For 10K racing though, once you're used to two miles at 5K speed, you can decrease the recovery period, and then increase the number of repetitions.

Once target pace is attained, aim to do more repetitions at that pace.

One aim of interval training is to get your body used to running fast for a long period. Interval work allows you to run extensive mileage volume at fast pace--without wearing yourself out. Achieve the target speed, then emphasize improving endurance at that speed. Your body sets the limit on the number of reps.

Training at 5K pace? Aim toward 10K of speedwork. Running at two mile speed? Aim for 6,000 meters.

When you increase the speed of your reps, more of each rep is anaerobic. As you get stronger; as your muscles get used to the new speed; as your body learns to process more oxygen, (helped by your steady runs), it becomes more aerobic. Over the months, the anaerobic training changes to aerobic training: You'll race faster.

You may find that while aiming for say 72 seconds, some of your efforts are closer to 70. If you make a conscious effort to run every fourth rep faster--that is, to intentionally run a 70--moving to 70s as your training pace will become easier. The occasional faster rep also helps to break up the session.

Avoid doing 400s or 300s week in, week out. Doing the same session repeatedly will only make you good at running that session. The 800s do something for you which the 400s won't. Don't miss out on their benefits.

Long Reps at VO2 Max.

Remember that physiologists agree the percentages at the higher level (100--95 %) should be done for 3-5 minutes' duration, repeated many times in one session--lets take a look at long VO2 max reps.

Long reps at VO2 max will keep you in oxygen debt for a greater percentage of your running time, giving the cardiovascular system and muscles more stimulation and encouragement to change.

> Interval training places greater mental strain on you because you concentrate on running form at high speed for 2 minutes or more at a time. It may also place you under more physical strain than you've been used to.

The Best Session.

The simplest way to improve VO2 max is long reps at 90 to 100 percent of max VO2. Alternate 1,000 meters at 2 mile pace, with miles at 5K pace, with 2,000s at 10K pace. This equates to 100, 95 and 90 percent of VO2 max. Most of you will want to run the 2Ks at 5 mile race pace. Though a mere one second per lap faster than 10K pace, at about 92 percent of VO2 max, it's a psychologically very important 4 seconds per mile faster than 10K pace. Few runners can accept actual 10K pace as the speed at which to train in preparation for a 10K.

If you've still not raced 5,000 meters, realize that elite runners run 2.5 seconds per lap faster for 5,000 meters compared to their 10,000 meter speed. Most runners should be able to run two to three seconds per lap faster for half the distance. If not, then run more reps at two mile pace, plus some training at mile pace. The 29 minute 10K runner speeds up by the same percentage that you should. His ten seconds per mile takes him to a 14 minute 5,000 meters.

Moving up from 5,000 meters.

Make sure you have the endurance to race within 2-3 seconds per lap of your 5K speed; within 12 seconds per mile. If you have problems, look to your:

Long runs for aerobic base.

Hills and anaerobic intervals for strength.

Long reps and lots of short reps for VO2 max endurance and lactate buffering capacity. Run 10 percent of your weekly miles in one interval session--the 10 percent excludes your warm-up and cooldown.

Run a Mixture of Training Sessions.

You may choose to run 1,000s at 5K pace every three weeks. Your second session could be 400s at 2 mile pace. Your third, a mixture of 300s and 600s or 800s.

The 17 sessions of each would give you a full year of progression. Reduce the recovery to 100 when running 300s; to 200 for your 600-800s. If you mix in a different, or guest session each month, you'll only run 12 sessions of 1,000s. giving you greater variety.

The first time through this training cycle, or the first time you do VO2 max training is likely to give you spectacular results. To your one minute gain from threshold pace running at the 10K you may be able to take another minute off your 10K with interval training. In your early running years, you can use the speed of your current 300s as your target for next year's 400s.

Be prepared for less significant gains in future years. VO2 max training will allow you to race close to your current fitness potential. Keep the speed of reps in proper relationship to your race pace. When racing 10Ks, there's little point in running faster than two mile pace. If 5,000 is your main goal, some mile pace interval running is prudent.

It takes relatively few 200s at your best 1,500 or mile speed to give the extra pep to your stride--and extra strength to your muscles--so run very few 200s for most of the year. Unless you're expecting Olympic gold, half a dozen 200s within a session of 400s should be sufficient. You will train close to mile pace when running 300s; these are much more stimulating to your anaerobic buffering system than 200s.

Like hamburger every session? Run the same distance every week?

You could run 400s every week--if you do them a different way each time.

Twenty reps at 10K pace with a fast 100 jog for strength; 16 reps at 5,000 pace with a slow 100 jog, and 12 at 2 mile pace with a fast 200 rest, would give a reasonable amount of VO2 max stimulation. Those paces give you 90 percent of VO2 max training through 100 percent. You would get even better VO2 results from including those long reps at 5K pace though.

Maverick again: Tired at Speed...Relax.

When you begin to lose form...when your running style goes...run several reps while fatigued. Any runner can run a fast quarter...just watch the start of most races. Few are efficient runners in the 16th or 22nd quarter of a 10K. Practice running at 5K pace when almost drained.

Race pace running with weary muscles, if practiced with good form, teaches you how to run fast in the middle to the end of a race. It will give you added confidence and improve your race day concentration.

Try a few one hundreds after a session of short reps, or a couple 400s after long reps--it's a great way to finish a session. Run relaxed with tired muscles.

It's also good preparation for when you increase the length of your interval session.

Don't sprint or rush. And don't make it hurt...much.

Keep speed sessions fun. Run in tranquil environments when possible. Avoid the distractions from people.

How Many Weeks for Intervals?

Many coaches argue that runners will make substantial improvements in running economy, but should only do 6 weeks of speedwork. They also say decrease mileage for these 6 weeks.

Studies have shown that runners who did intervals every day for 6 days before a race, while cutting mileage by 85 percent, race faster. The typical study is along the lines of five times 400 at the beginning of the week...decreasing to one rep at the end of the taper. Participants might improve their race performance by 8 seconds per mile.

That's a wonderful pace increase--worth about 50 seconds for a 10K.

However...the runner who is new to interval training makes these same huge gains in running economy when introducing any speed session. Most runners striding out their 200, 300 and 400s for the first time find it very easy to up their 400 meter pace by 2-3 seconds per lap after just two sessions. This alone would account for more than the 8 seconds per mile race improvement.

A reduction in training by such a proportion, would also (on its own), give a substantial boost to race times.

Are the improved race times due to rest or intervals?

Both of course.

After all, if you'd never done speedwork before, the gains will be enormous; add the resting up...you're bound to get faster.

Most of those studies take a group of runners who have done steady running for only about 10 weeks to develop base. They don't take a group of runners who have run fartlek, hills and anaerobic threshold pace training for half a year...because their gains would be more modest. You already have good running economy from other types of speedwork, and a high VO2 max. You are now easing an extra bit of VO2 max and running efficiency into your body. This takes time.

Save the resting and peaking for Chapter Five. Keep your mileage and long runs during this phase or you'll lose your base aerobic capacity and strength.

For now, just like those 300 and 400s after a threshold run in Chapter Three, practice good running economy on moderately tired legs.

Besides, why would you want to stop interval training after only six weeks. You've just got used to the session, your running economy has improved, yet we keep seeing training programs which say do only six weeks. Just when you're beginning to benefit from reps, they say stop. Yet runners are capable of running, enjoying, and benefiting from track sessions year round.

Ignore the six weeks, then take a break idea. Improve your endurance by adding more reps. Get away from the track for a few weeks twice a year, but continue fast running elsewhere to keep your hard-earned good form.

Run the same training session regularly, at the same fitness level, and your times will vary according to how tired you are, (mental or physical), your food intake and hydration status, and the weather. Run at your planned heartrate goal, not your pace goal. Don't worry about the times changing, but try to find the reason for your fast days. Repeat these ideal conditions for your race days.

You Don't Need Pain.

While a little discomfort is good for you because it indicates a modest degree of intensity, only the last quarter of your reps should feel hard: it's these harsh feeling reps which will make you stronger.

Get through your interval sessions by thinking about running form on each rep. Run each rep, and the entire session at appropriate pace--a pace which allows you to run well the next day. Your next day should be a long run--unless you follow a regime which dictates that a long run should be preceded by a rest day.

Your longest run is a third to less than a quarter of your average weekly mileage. You run it at an easy pace. The ideal is to run a full speed session on Saturday...then follow it with the long *recovery* run on Sunday.

VO2 Max Training in Operation.

Let's say you're a 16 minute 5K runner. At the track is a group of 15:25 to 15:35 runners. When they run miles at 5K pace, you can do 800s at the same pace--but you'll be at 3,000 pace. You could also run a 600, rest while they do the middle lap, then do a second 600. Sometimes you can set the pace for them--try to make it even pace. Or, join in at the back of the group. When they do 400s at 3K pace, you can do 300s at close to mile pace.

Post speedwork you're after a pleasant, satisfying tired feeling. Feel completely stuffed after an easy mile and a shower? You probably ran the session too fast, or it was too much volume for your current fitness level. Achy muscles for *days* post VO2 max session is overtraining.

Speed Table 15:30 5K (4:30 mile, 9:38 two mile, 32 for 10K).

Both types of intervals improve VO2 Maximum.

	The Short reps Improve mainly Aerobic ability			The Long reps Improve mainly Anaerobic buffering		
Reps of	200	300	400	400	800	mile
Recovery	200	200	200	400	800	800
Race pace	mile	2m	5K	mile	2m	5K
Rep speed	34	54	74	70	2:24	4:56
# of reps	16	15	16	4	3	2
Build to	24+	20+	20+	8	4+	3+
See	*Note one*			*Note two*		

Note One...You have to set the limit on the number of reps. You can ignore the 10 percent mileage rule. Rest up to peak with a five mile training session. Or, ease through more reps at 10 to 12 seconds per mile slower (10K pace). Try quarters in 77 and 300s in 56--which is 90 percent of VO2 max--though half the reps should still be close to 5K pace. Run the second half of your intervals faster, or alternate a 5K pace with a 10K pace rep. When you've done a particular session three or four times, ease more of the reps toward 5K pace.

You can combine the sessions once a month. Eight each at 400, 300, and 200 gives four and a half miles. You speed from 5K to one mile pace as rep distance decreases. Aim eventually for a one hundred jog.

Note Two...these 400s will be more anaerobic, more stimulating. Same for the 800s at two mile pace, and the

miles at 5K pace. You'll need longer rest due to the distance run at these speeds. Alternate:
   * the three sessions between track and other surfaces
   * the three distances
   * each session of long reps with one of short reps
   Also, remember your anaerobic threshold sessions.
Final note...This table is based on a 15:24 to 15:30 5K runner. For the rest of you, your reps should be 3 seconds per lap faster than 10K pace to represent 5,000 pace; 5 secs a lap faster than 10K pace to equal your two mile potential; 10 seconds per lap faster than 10K to match the one mile.
   If in doubt...do any reps faster than the pace you intend to race at...10 to 15 seconds per mile faster...it's that simple.

The VO2 Max Pace Chart on page 92 is based on 2 mile and 5K times, which gives 100 or 95 percent of VO2 max. Your mile PR and 10K PR should be on the same line.

   If the 400s feel easy, but you have difficulty maintaining pace on the 800 and 1,200s, you lack background base endurance. Run more miles at 70 percent max HR to build base aerobic ability.
   If the 400s feel harsh, incorporate 100s etc., to work on form at speed. Then run some 200s and 300s before trying the 400s again. Relaxed running at 2 mile pace takes practice. Don't let 400s dominate; you can run 800s at 2 mile pace also. The 1,200s may be the most under used session. You can also run mile reps at either pace.

VO2 Max training pace based on 2 mile and 5K race times...100 and 95 percent VO2 max.

MILE PR	Time for 2 mile	two mile VO2 400s	5 K (VO2) 800s	5 K Time 3.1m	5K (VO2) 1,200s	10 k 6.21m
4:20	9:19	69.8	2:23.6	14:57	3:35	30:54
4:30	9:40	72.5	2:29.0	15:31	3:44	32:02
4:40	10:02	75.2	2:34.4	16:05	3:52	33:10
4:50	10:23	77.9	2:39.8	16:39	4:00	34:20
5:00	10:44	80.5	2:45.0	17:11	4:08	35:27
5:10	11:06	83.2	2:50.4	17:45	4:16	36:37
5:20	11:28	86	2:56.0	18:20	4:24	37:50
5:30	11:50	88.7	3:01.4	18:54	4:32	39:00
5:40	12:11	91.4	3:06.8	19:27	4:40	40:09
5:50	12:32	94	3.12.0	20:00	4:48	41:15
6:00	12:54	96.7	3:17.4	20:34	4:56	42:23
6:10	13:15	99.4	3:22.8	21:07	5:04	43:29
6:20	13:37	102.1	3:28.2	21:41	5:12	44:40
6:30	14:00	105	3:34.0	22:18	5:20	45:56
6:45	14:31	108.9	3:41.8	23:06	5:33	47:35
7:00	15:03	112.9	3:49.8	23:56	5:45	49:18
7:15	15:35	116.9	3:57.8	24:46	5:57	50:41
7:30	16:07	120.9	4:05.8	25:36	6:09	52:44
7:45	16:40	125	4:15.0	26:33	6:22	54:41
8:00	17:12	129	4:23.0	27:24	6:34	56:26
8:30	18:16	137	4:39.0	29:10	7:00	60:06
9:00	19:01	142.6	4:54.0	30:25	7:21	62:42
10:00	21:30	161.2	5:23.0	33:36	8:03	69:16

CHAPTER FIVE

5K & 10K PEAKING

You've already done:
Intervals at VO2 Max, Anaerobic Threshold
Hills & Strength Training, Base Mileage & Fartlek

While rest is important when peaking for a race, there are some special speed sessions which can further improve your race times. These sessions will fine tune your running skill; these short workouts will keep your legs energized and fresh, ready for the big race.

The serious runner who follows this program for the first time can decrease mileage by 20 percent per week for four weeks, while running a few VO2 max sessions at 2 mile pace instead of 5K pace. The moderate to severe intensity runners, or people going through this scheme for a second time may linger here for 10 weeks...honing their ability to run at 2 mile race pace with very long reps. Their mileage decrease should wait until the last few weeks.

Whichever group you belong to, the 2 mile pace running will enable you to tolerate higher levels of lactic acid in your body, and make you buffer wastes still better than in phase four. You will also feel more relaxed at high speed, while making additional muscle strength gains. The lower mileage will give freshness to your step--provided you have a solid mileage base.

According to coach Janos Ronaszeki, "You cannot run hard without base...the injury risk is too great." Sessions of long reps at 2 mile pace are definitely hard running. You need the base mileage and strength from the first three chapters, plus the basic intervals from Chapter Four before you run long reps at 2 mile speed.

Some of these sessions will improve your sprinting ability by bringing in the last of your fast twitch muscle fibers. The goal, however, is to improve your average running pace, not your end sprint. If you possess an exceptional sprint at the end of your 10K or 5K race, it could mean you did not run hard enough in the rest of the race. Many runners slow in the third quarter of a 10K. Make a special effort to run miles four and five at fast pace; run slightly faster than the third mile. Don't save much for that last mile and a quarter.

You will have raced at least five 10Ks by now, so you've had a chance to experiment with modest starts where you speed up, and with even paced racing. The same at 5,000 meters. If you did any of those 5Ks on the track, you may have experienced the tendency that runners have of relaxing but slowing at 3,000 meters. The 3K point has special significance--it's a race distance itself. You do need to run relaxed in the 4th 1,000 but don't slow down. It is better to speed up by half a second per lap. Don't save much for the end of the race. This chapter will help you to run at a faster even pace; it will help you to personal records.

We will look at the lingering section later. First the two sessions which all of you should run in the last 4-6 weeks to:

Peak for 10K and 5K Racing.

These two sessions will take your training to a new level. Three times 1,000 meters at one second per lap faster than 2 mile pace with 7-8 minutes rest is a good substitute for a 3,000 meter or two mile race. Three times a mile at two mile pace with similar rest does wonders for those rarely racing at 5K. Both sessions, or the use of 5,000 meter racing are great preparation for 10K racing.

Most runners at a big race don't compete in track races. Long reps at high VO2 max effort give the same advantages track circuit stars have. They typically alternate 3,000 and 5,000 meter races; or use one or two of each to prepare for a 10,000. So can you.

Pick a 10K race and run your own variation of these sessions every 7-10 days.

* *5 x 800 meters at one second per lap faster than 2 mile pace*
* 4 x 1,200 meters at two mile pace
* *6 x 800 meters at faster than 2 mile pace*
* 3 x one mile at two mile pace
* *4 x 1,000 meters at faster than 2 mile pace*
* 3 x one mile at 2 mile pace
* *4 x 1,000 at faster than 2 mile pace*
* Race 5,000 meters, or run 3 x one mile at 5K pace

* *4 x 1,000 at two mile pace*
* The big 5K or 10K race

Only run these long reps at or faster than 2 mile pace if you've already done reps of 600 meters as described in Chapter Four. Support each session of long reps with two other speed sessions. The first session would be short reps at 2 mile to 5K pace. Run them as hill reps once every three weeks for knee lift and to maintain strength...and to get you away from the track. The other session will be at 15K pace.

Make Three Attempts at each session before progressing further.

According to Harry Wilson, the British Amateur Athletic Board Coach who guided Olympic contenders at 10,000 meters, plus Steve Ovett to Gold medals at 800 to 5,000 meters, and the world best at two miles.

"Athletes usually need three attempts at a session before they can progress further. The first is an introduction--the second time is coming to terms--the third time is being in charge of the session...that's the time to move forward.

"During the last few sessions as you approach big races, you are not trying to run faster than before--you are trying to match your previous time...but in a more relaxed way. At the end of the session you should feel, Hey, if I'd wanted to, I could run that session faster."

Two mile pace training increases your maximum oxygen assimilation ability. You'll race faster.

Practice running the second and third session of miles with good form--keep the running as effortless as possible. You'll know that you can run the session because you've done it before; think about completing the session in comfort.

As Harry Wilson suggests, run three sessions of miles and thousands to peak for your 5K or 10K race. Note the top of page 96--you run the last session of miles and 1,000s at a slower pace as you approach your race. This makes it still easier for you to relax rather than strain your way toward the race.

Pay attention to your body. Top runners associate with the discomforts of fast running. Feel like slowing because it's hard work to keep your pace? Think about form and relaxation of all your muscles; think about your position in relation to the ground. Relax your way through the second half of the (mile, or the 5K) run.

Fresh Legs.

You should run these long reps with fresh legs, after an easy run or rest day. Wear lightweight shoes to put you in the mood to go fast. Start modestly--run longer reps as you progress. At the track, unless you're doing a speed effort, stay out of the inside lanes. If you're doing a fast rep...faster runners must go around you.

Short intervals and anaerobic threshold (bread and butter) sessions, can be run on tired legs--provided you've used the build-up starting in Chapter One! Even in this peaking phase, you retain some sessions from each of the first four chapters.

Don't Reduce Mileage too Soon.

Unless you run more than 60 per week, you should avoid reducing your mileage until the last three weeks. It only takes 12-21 days to lose half of your aerobic fitness when you are not running much. Your blood volume decreases, further compromising your racing. Don't lose months of strength and endurance running by cutting back too early. Running magazines quote studies showing you can maintain 90 percent of fitness during prolonged spells at low mileage. Your aim is to maintain 100 percent of your hard earned fitness. Don't de-train while running these long reps.

Low mileage runners should consider longer repetitions. According to Wilson, "The person who runs 4 one mile repeats at goal 5K pace, is more likely to race a 5K at that pace, than the person who runs 4 miles worth of 1,000 meter reps at 5K pace. It's not just how high you raise the heartrate, but also how long you can maintain it at a steady high level."

Long fast repetitions will take your heartrate to very near its maximum level, about 170-200 beats per minute, by the end of each fast rep. Your HR should drop to 110-120 before you begin the next repetition.

Running the 1,000s faster than 2 mile pace will mean training at 102-105 percent of VO2 max.

Racing flats for 3K or faster training make you feel lighter. Do warm and stretch the calf and Achilles. See page 42. Warm muscles are more efficient, less likely to strain. Speedwork can then be done with minimal injury risk from the lower heel on these shoes.

Eight Ways to Greater Speed.

For the lingerers--definitely not malingerers, here are eight other running sessions to prepare you for peaking--or to gain more legspeed at any stage of your training.

1. Stride and Coast.

Run sprints of about fifty meters, but with a fast fifty meter jog recovery. You could start with a mile of this running; build to three miles as you get used to them--which will give you 1.5 fast miles. This is similar to the fartlek of 40 weeks ago, or the bends and straights in preparation for interval training. Now though, in addition to the efforts being fast, the rest period must be fast. Don't allow your muscles to recover completely. This session develops speed and will help you cover an opponents race burst.

Run it as a sprint...coast...sprint...coast. Don't ease to a jog at the end of each stride. The six minute mile 10K runner should be sprinting at 5:30 pace and coasting at 7:00 pace.

The 'coasting' section does not last many seconds--but nor does the fast part. The cumulative effect after a mile, or sixteen of these efforts is your goal. Your net pace is close to tempo run speed, yet you'll be working more of the fast twitch muscle fibers.

> Don't neglect strength training during this speed phase. Racing months need resistance training. Don't do them as often, but maintain your earlier strength gains.

2. Sprint Drills.

You should have been working on running form in week one of your training. That was the purpose of the form hints and fartlek in Chapter One. Now you can run some 150 meter strides working on a relaxed, fast running action. Speed up in five stages every ten meters; maintain maximum speed for fifty meters or so, then run out (ease down), over the last fifty meters. Run these drills on well groomed grass if possible.

Lean forward while staying tall. Run off your whole forefoot and give a final push from the toes. Reduce wasted motion...keep the head still. Feel the surface, pull the surface back to you and devour the ground. Push off from the toes with full leg extension--at the hip and in the calf muscles.

Practice strides as a separate session; later, do six acceleration runs at the end of a weekly track session.

3. Speed during the Long Run.

Bring in your fast twitch muscle fibers on every SECOND or THIRD long run. About two miles from the end of some runs, change up to 15K race pace for half a mile--two times a quarter, or four times 200 meters works just as well. Run the fast part relaxed; then cruise in the last part of the run.

4. Differentials.

The differential involves splitting an interval into two parts. Run the first part at 10K pace to take the stuffing out of your legs: Then, accelerate pace by four or five seconds per 400 meters--to about 2 mile race pace. Do fewer efforts with longer recovery than in an even paced session. For example:

8 x 800 in 2 min 30 secs with half lap jog could become 6 x 800 with the first lap 77 secs, and the second lap 73 secs; take a full lap jog.

12 x 400 in 72 secs with half lap jog become 8 x 400 split 37/35, with a full lap jog.

5. Downhills.

Running up a slight hill costs almost twice as much energy as you gain coming down that hill. Practice both ways with relaxed form.

Remember from Chapter Two--downhills teach you relaxation. Practice good form with fast leg turnover. Run perpendicular to the slope--work the arms to increase leg speed and stride. Run downhill reps of 200 to 400 meters. Spring off your calf at maximum leg speed. Swing those feet through close to your buttocks.

Start with two or three efforts...increase the number as your buttocks, hamstrings and calves become used to the effort and speed. This session gives the soleus muscle a bonus workout.

6. Wind.

You can do long reps with the wind to help your legspeed, or while resting up pre-race.

To improve legspeed, run the reps at what you consider to be your normal intensity...at long rep heartrate for those who use a monitor, while letting the wind push you to a faster pace. Stay relaxed though, or you will lose the benefit. Running with the wind can give you 2 mile (or faster) legspeed at 5K effort.

Pre-race, you can also run at your usual pace, but the effort will be easier because you'll be pushed by the wind. Jog back into the wind at easy effort.

7. Lactate Buffering.

When you've got more racing experience, you can break a session into sets. Run 300s a second faster than you've been doing them, but take shorter recoveries.

Start with two 300s, and take a fast 100 recovery between the reps. This pair is a set. Run a lap of the track as extra rest prior to another set of 300s.

The first effort will seem easy; maintaining pace on the second and third 300 gets progressively harder.

For the best training effect, the last 300 should be as fast, or one second faster than the first. When you've done this session successfully a couple of times, you can try sets of three, four, then five reps. Five reps will simulate a mile race. Don't do more than three miles of these intervals in a session.

Due to the short recovery, your muscle lactate levels remains high. This increases your anaerobic capacity and lactate tolerance...the amount of lactate your muscles can hold before forcing you to slow down. Increasing lactate holding capacity allows you to maintain high speeds longer.

Exercise physiologists call it increasing your 'buffering system' or 'buffering capacity.' Like running at two mile pace, you breathe deeper, thus increasing the maximum quantity of oxygen your lungs can take in, and which your blood has the opportunity to absorb. You can also run 200s with an even shorter rest if you intend to race at 2 miles--30 seconds rest is ideal.

8. Still Faster...but Shorter.

Acceleration sessions add variety and are a time efficient substitute to avoid traveling to a mile race.
800 meters at mile pace (110 % VO2 max) is a good way to start the session...take a five minute recovery.
600 meters just a bit faster...take a full recovery.
Then run a 400 and a 300 at 800 race pace. You should only need about three minutes rest between each.

You can use short reps for bulky acceleration sessions like 1984 Olympic Gold Medalist at 10,000 meters, Alberto Cova. He did 500s, 400s, 300s and 200s. He took a 100 jog between everything, but did not run them as sets! His pace came down from 5,000 race speed to mile pace for the 200s.

Run these drills and efficiency enhancers with fresh legs in order to run them fast. Keep your steady runs easy to allow recovery between speed sessions.

> Running is more productive as it becomes more efficient. Efficiency equates to fast running.

Two Big Races.

Some people get good success with the double peak system. They rest up while finessing speed for a race--then take another easy week before racing again.

Most of the six or seven days between races will be easy runs of three to four miles...provided it's half or less of the athletes normal day. The sub 30 mile a week person will not run on these rest days.

Two days after the race would be a long run; do 60-75 percent of your normal long run.

Four days after the race would also be three days before the next race, so:
Run at 2 mile pace. Cruise an 800; then some 300-400s, and finish with another 800. Then race again. You can repeat this week three or four times before going back to base training. Make some variation to your one speed session though.

Racing more than Twice.

You can race well for 6 to 8 consecutive weeks. Simply run enough quality to stay fast, with sufficient mileage to maintain strength, and enough rest to keep fresh.

The day after a five or ten kilometer race you can run long but easy--at 70 percent of max heartrate. This is a relaxing way to get the race out of the system, while maintaining your aerobic base. But not too much mileage. A 12 instead of a 15 will suffice.

Then you have three days to do some useful training before resting up for the next race. Short intervals or fartlek, and long repetitions will be ideal. Run three quarters or less of your usual quantity: Like 10 x 600? Run 3 x 600 to start, then 4 x 200-300, and finish with three more 600s. Work on form. Allow your body to recover between race efforts. Split the two quality sessions with a midweek easy run for aerobic stamina.

Weekly Racing Schedule.

Motto. Persevere with speed sessions while heavy legged. Then rest towards the end of the week.

Day one -- Race.

Day two -- Recovery run -- ten or twelve miles should suffice.

Day three -- Fartlek -- including a few hill strides, or an interval session of 200 to 400 meters.

Day four -- a nice midweek 55 min run at easy to steady pace.

Day five -- long reps. Instead of three times one mile at 2 mile pace, run a mile at 5K pace, then 3-4 times 300 meters at 2 mile pace, then a second mile at 5K pace. Stay relaxed.

Alternate this session with 1,000 meters at two mile pace. Take a break with 6 gentle 200s just a little faster, and finish with another 1,000 at 2 mile pace.

Check your pace judgment and running form with these sessions. As coach Wilson suggested on page 96, your goal here is not to improve fitness...it's simply to maintain fitness while relaxing at pace.

Day six and seven - Easy run of up to forty mins.

You can switch days three and five. Don't run the short reps faster than 2 mile pace. Simply cruise through these intervals. Put more effort into your form than the actual speed. You'll be fast because you are fit. Unless you work on running technique during these weeks, the training will wear you down rather than relaxing you for the next race. Besides, this running will not help you in the coming weekend's race, yet it can compromise this weekend's race...if you run too hard. Its training effect, however, should aid you in next week's race.

You can still train at 15K pace. Three times one mile should seem like a rest day--but it will maintain your anaerobic threshold gains from Chapter Three.

Moderate intensity runners may find one speed session between races is sufficient. Serious runners may simply run a dozen relaxed strides or a gentle fartlek midweek, and a couple of easy runs.

You often feel worse the second day post-race as your muscles go through the healing process. It takes confidence in your body to take it through the modest interval session on day three--you may feel stiffer than you did a few minutes after the race. Yet this modest session, followed by days four and five, will give the muscles enough active rest to keep you racing fit. The four easy days each week will enable you to race well for months, but then you should back-off from racing. Race once a month for a spell; use races at the end of an easy week, while you're back in base training.

The Perfect Race.

Running your perfect 5K or 10K race requires practice with short races, long reps at one and two mile pace, and rest. Quite a long rest--which is probably the most important aspect of peaking for a superb performance.

> Think of yourself as powerful and energetic during interval training. Imagine strong, graceful animals...including your favorite runners.

In addition to running 10-15 percent less mileage for a few weeks while practicing those fast reps, you will decrease by 20, 40, 60 and 80 percent...four phases lasting one to four days each.

Take the 40 Mile a Week Runner.

The weekend speed session--cut it down by half a mile. 1,000s or 800 meters at two mile pace with long rest would be good.

The weekend long run--20 percent shorter than your typical run--run 10 seconds per mile slower than usual, on an easier course, at a cooler time of day.

Monday, run a half speed session (five 400s instead of ten).

Wednesday, run ten relaxed 100-200s.

If you run one speed session midweek, try 3 x 400 and 3 x 200 and 2 x 100.

Shorten the midweek medium run to an easy 4 miles.

And at 70 Miles Per Week.

Decreasing mileage in steps is more significant for high mileage people. Every three days, decrease mileage by 20 percent.

Run eight miles for three days; then six for three days and four on the last three days pre-race. Factor in your weekly long run, and the last fourteen days of our seventy weeker, would change from the usual week of, 10, 15, 9, 11, 8, 9, 6. To become: 9, 12, 9, 8, 8, 8, 6, (a 60 mile week). Then 6, 10, 6, 6, 4, 4, 4 (40 miles). Retain fast running on your usual days.

The first week had three miles taken off the longest and second longest runs--13 and 11 days pre-race. Factor in the speed sessions being reduced by a mile, and by day seven, your leg muscles should be feeling fresh. Seven days prior to the race is a chance to run three miles of good speedwork at 2 mile to 5K pace, or a 5K tempo. Don't overdo the pace.

Six days pre-race, if you must go for double digits, don't go over ten miles.

There are just enough miles on day five and three pre-race to run 4 times 800 meters and 4 times 400 meters respectively.

Peaking is best done with a combination of reduced overall mileage, and a reduction in the amount of speed running--though some runners like to saunter through the speedwork a second or two per lap faster.

You can reduce your mileage by 15 to 20 percent for three to four weeks, finishing with about 40 percent of your regular miles. For example, an 80 mile a week person could run 65, 55 and 40.

You can simply take a mile off each of your runs until you get down to say four miles for the last three days pre-race. If you average seven miles a day, you would need to commence the taper 6 days pre-race. A better taper would be achieved by coming down a mile every two or three days. Just like your muscles took time to adapt to the increased training many months prior to this peaking, your body takes time to fully utilize the rest. This is partly because you can now relax during your long reps at two mile pace.

Speedwork Order.

How you organize your speedwork to peak is important yet personal. As mileage decreases, the length of the reps should decrease. The race pace you train at will decrease--legspeed increases. The last four sessions, done at two to four day intervals according to the schedule you've been used to, might be:

* miles, 1,000s, 600s, and 300s.
* The pace will probably be 15K, 5K, 2 mile and one mile.
* The total amount of reps for the high mileage runner might be 5, 4, 3 and 2 miles.

Of course, you can rest up with the opposite approach. Run long reps at fast pace early...then drop to short reps at slower pace. The last four speed sessions could be:

* 3 x one mile at 2 mile pace
* 4 x 1,000 meters at 5K pace
* 5 x 600 meters at 10K pace
* 6 x 400 at 15K pace

This technique would avoid burnout just before a race. The first session, the mile reps at two mile pace is harsh; the others get progressively easier. All runners possess a natural fastest speed; running the last two sessions are slower than 5K pace will not stop you from racing at 5K pace. Actually, your legs will be well rested to race at 5,000 meters. Your muscles will be fresh because you cruised through the last two sessions.

Note how the amount of fast running comes down from three miles to only one-and-a-half miles per session at the end. Because you're running slower, you could run three miles at each pace, such as 12 times 400 meters at 15K pace for the last session, and you would still be resting up. For psychological reasons, and to bring in those fast twitch muscle fibers, finish the 15K pace session with four 100s at mile pace. Mile pace is fast, but far from flat out speed. This short session should not exhaust you.

5K or 10K Racing.

This author makes no mileage concession to 5,000 meter runners: you need just as much strength and endurance from mileage as a 10K runner. Don't be bashful about running high mileage; you need the aerobic base to race well at 5K.

This author also gives no speedwork concession to 10,000 meter runners: you need just as much speed and VO2 max stimulation and economical running practice as a 5K runner.

The only difference to your training is that a 10K runner can get away without training faster than 2 mile pace (100 percent VO2 max). The 5K specialist should benefit more from training sessions at mile pace. All of you need to retain base aerobic endurance.

There's no single session to take your personal records down, but resting up, combined with the speed sessions above should help you race faster.

The most important thing is to rest, while doing sufficient running that you do not de-train.

CHAPTER SIX

RACING at
RELATED DISTANCES

Training for the 2 Mile, the 5 Mile, the 12 Kilometer, 10 Miles and Half-Marathon.

Two Mile or 3,000 Meter Racing.

The Two Mile is great preparation for 5K racing. You will already have been training at two mile pace or 100 percent of VO2 max. Now, because you should train at the race distance shorter than your target race, you'll need to do a significant amount of running at mile pace.

You did 5K pace running to prepare for 10K racing. You did 3K pace training prior to those 5,000s. Now is the time for faster training at 110 percent of your VO2 Maximum. Run about one and a half times race distance at mile pace during an Interval session. Try:

Running a dozen 200s at mile pace during your 3K pace sessions a couple of times to prepare you for:

First - The Basic.

12-16 times 400 meters at four to five seconds per lap faster than 3,000 meter pace--or seven seconds per lap faster than 5K pace. This is not all that fast considering how strong your legs should be from 5K and 10K training. The fourth or seventh rep may seem fast if you don't give yourself sufficient rest between reps. A lap of relatively fast easy running should be best. If your long runs are 7 minutes per mile, jog at 8 minute miles for this recovery. This gives you a two minute rest.

Second - The Softer Option. But not too soft.

Run 300s at mile pace. Practice these in sets. Run three to four reps with a 30-45 second rest between them. Take an extra lap after each set. Amass three miles at speed, but only at mile pace. Faster than mile speed is likely to burn you out; training at mile speed develops stronger muscles.

And, Finally.

Long reps at mile pace. 8 X 600, or if you're really bold, 6 X 800. You'll deserve a full recovery after each rep. Take three to five minutes.

Take a look back at Chapter Five for Acceleration sessions and other options. Don't forget differentials either. One lap at 3K pace followed by a lap at mile pace will give you many benefits of an entire 800 at mile pace.

This 110 percent VO2 max training further increases your lactate buffering capacity. Running each type of session three times at 5-7 day intervals will give you a 7-9 week preparation. Rest appropriately and you'll be ready for a superb 3,000 meter or 2 mile race.

Don't decrease your mileage until just before your 2 mile race--you still need aerobic base. Retain the 95 percent VO2 max sessions (5K pace), anaerobic threshold work, and the hills to maintain your strength endurance.

8K or 5 Mile Race Training.

One of the best ways to train for a race is to run the entire race distance as intervals. Hardly a serious problem when preparing for a 5,000 meter race. However, most runners find ten kilometers of speedwork or track intervals intolerable. The eight kilometer or the five mile race allows you to complete the entire race distance in an interval training session more easily. Run the 5 miles of reps at close to maximum VO2--5K race pace.

Strictly speaking, 100 percent VO2 max is two mile race pace, a pace you should certainly train at for 5K racing. One blessing of training for the 8K and beyond is you can run most of your interval training at 5K race pace--which is 95 percent of VO2 max. You will still be running 5-10 seconds per mile faster than race pace.

The only caveat to doing 8K of speedwork is that it must either:

Be 10 percent or less of your average weekly distance training; or, be treated as a substitute for a race--you rest up to run the session.

Even then, don't race to take great chunks off your fastest time for the session. Running relaxed at 5K pace is better than uncontrolled sprinting at mile pace. Within the first half mile of the warmdown, your legs should still feel re-energized. The life should already be coming back.

Don't turn off the pain during these long sessions. Pain warns you to slow down. Don't mask the pain with pills, or you will lose the body's warning sign to stop exercising. Ignore pain at your peril, or you will get what you deserve...a long break from running.

8K of VO2 Max Interval Training.

Lets ignore 400s and short efforts. Many runners tend to over-emphasize quarters. Though you will be doing 400s, they were covered in Chapter Four and in the 3K training above. The three interval sessions for this section are...breathe deeply now.

4 x 2,000 meters with 5-7 minute rest;
5 x one mile repeat with 3-5 minute rest intervals; and,
8 x 1,000 meters with 2-3 minutes rest.

These track sessions would be easy at 15K or 10 mile race pace, but are quite demanding at 5K pace. Your steady runs, your long runs, will have done wonders for your VO2 max. This running of long reps at 95 percent of maximum oxygen uptake capacity will take you to a new level--provided you:

Don't run VO2 Max Long Interval Training too often.
Every ten days is best for most of us. Three times a month allows you to do each session 12 times a year. Not always on the track though. Long reps up-hill or on a soft surface for resistance training will combine two types of training.

Which Pace?
Runners on high mileage might run these interval sessions at 2 mile pace, or 100 percent VO2 max. Most of you will

find 5K pace plenty hard enough. Long reps at two mile pace was discussed extensively in Chapter Five.

You can cheat your Heart and Lungs though.
If you have a longish section of smooth grass at one to two percent grade, run downhill at 5-10 seconds faster than 5K pace...which will be two mile race pace. Your heart--your entire cardiorespiratory system--will only be working at around 5K effort level. It's the opposite for those up-hill reps. If your legs are at 5K speed, your heart will be at 2 mile intensity. See page 38 for details.

The pace to run your VO2 max intervals is current 5K race pace, not your dream pace. This will be 10 to 15 seconds per mile faster than recent 10K pace.

Think about your running form during these track and other surface intervals. Though it's difficult to run this fast without decent form, it is your chance to correct little faults. See page 10.

Questioning the Five Training Phases.
"Do I have to follow the mileage build-up which you suggest?"

In Chapter One, I wrote that you could continue with your interval training as you increase mileage. You could simply add mileage to the four training elements in turn.

Lets see how it would work when moving from 40 up to 50 miles per week. Schedules are on page 140 and 150.

At 40 per week, the long run will be 13, but at 50 it can be 15.

Add two miles to each of your easy midweek runs for endurance, strength and improved aerobic ability, and you've already got 46.

After six weeks at 46, add a mile to your fartlek and hill sessions; four weeks later, add a mile to your threshold pace run. After another four weeks, increase your VO2 max session from 4 to 5 miles; add a mile to your warmdown to give you 50 mile weeks.

Six weeks of the lengthened VO2 max session will take you to your twentieth 15 miler--you should be close to your full athletic potential at 50 per week. It will be time to rest up for a race or two.

Running a few two mile pace sessions to help you peak, plus resting up, gives you a half year of training since your mileage increase. You can stay with the same training for several months to reach your full potential at 50 miles per week. Or:

1. Add more mileage.

2. Improve the quality or speed of some of your current fifty miles--see below.

Here's how quality training with 1,200s might progress over one year. It assumes you run them once a month. In winter, half the sessions will be away from the track.

Most time goals are arbitrary--a particular minute barrier or pace. Here, our runner does 39:30 for 10K; her goal is to get under 39 minutes--and perhaps break 6:10 per mile pace for the distance, or 38:19.

Six minutes per mile will represent her 5K pace next year. With these 1,200s she will train at close to current two mile pace early on--if she winters well, it becomes her 5,000 pace.

This runner is training at dream pace, (see page 115), not her current 5K speed. However, many of her mid-winter sessions are closer to current 5K pace.

Month...One   4 x 1,000 in 3:45 (90 per lap) with 600
    rest...gets you used to it.
Two   4 x 1,200 in 4:30 with 600 rest.
Three   5 x 1,200 in 4:36 (92 laps) with 400 rest.
Four   2 x 1,200 in 4:30; 3 x 800 in 3:00 with 400 rest.
Five   5 x 1,200 in 4:33 (91s) with 400 rest.
Six   3 x 1,200 and 2 x 800 at 90 per lap with 400 rest.
Seven   6 x 1,200 in 4:36, alternate 400 and 200 rests.
Eight   4 x 1,200 in 4:30 with 400 rest.
Nine   5 x 1,200 in 4:33 take a 400 rest. Run the last
    couple close to 4:30.
Ten   6 x 1,200 in 4:36, alternate 400 and 200 rests.
Eleven 5 x 1,200 in 4:32 (twice), 4:30 (3 reps), 400 rest.
Twelve 6 x 1,200 in 4:34, 4:32, 4:30 (twice), 4:28
    (twice) with 400 rest.

Speed goals are adjusted when the rest interval is decreased. You might choose to run 1,200s every three weeks. Other sessions could be 400s and 600s or 800s.

Both sexes race 5K and 10K. Yet most college training schedules show females running fewer reps of shorter distances than male runners. Women might run 6 x 800 meters while the men run 7 x 1,000. Surprised they can't race a 5K at their 800 rep pace? They're destined to failure. If your friend runs the same time as you for 5K or 10K, make sure you run longer reps than he or she does; run them at 5K to 2 mile pace. See page 98.

She could simply run 4 x 1,200 each month at the beginning of the season, but add an extra 400 meter rep at the same pace each session. After three months, she'd be doing the four 1,200s plus three 400s. Month four could be an 800 plus a 400; the fifth month would be five reps of 1,200. Repeating the process with the 400s will allow her to reach six 1,200s after ten sessions.

> Build whole body anatomic and physiologic strength before advancing to the next training level. Cross-train.

12 Kilometer Training.

I see no reason to change this essay from pages 125 and 126 of Running Dialogue.

12 KILOMETER TRAINING SCHEDULE.

If you've raced several 10 kilometer events there's nothing special about a 12K: Simply run close to your best at 10K...and keep going another mile and a quarter. Your last effort (the sprint), will have to wait an extra mile and a quarter. Because the middle part of the race will be longer, it becomes more important to spread your effort over the entire race.

We could increase your training by 20 percent to help you to a better time, but that would be like telling you to double your mileage before entering a 20K or half-marathon.

Instead, tweak your current mileage--adjust two runs.

First...the long run. If it's less than 10 miles, increase it by two miles. That's it. Run the same leisurely 70 percent of max heartrate pace, but for an extra 14 to 20 minutes. Steal these miles from one of your easy runs.

Second...the main speed session. If you've been used to three times one mile (or 1,600 meters), run an extra lap of the track to make 2,000s. Run at the same pace, but with a longer recovery the first few times. You can also change a session of six 800s to six 1,000s.

The weeks when your short stuff is the main session, either do another mile of them, or do more of them at the fast pace. Take 400s. You can break up a session by inserting 8 x 200 a tad faster than the sets of 400s each side. Many people find 16 x 400 is too close to a cure for insomnia; the 200s will entertain you. Or, instead of 12 x 400 with every fourth effort being run two seconds faster, run alternate reps faster.

Your mileage will be the same, but the borrowed miles will mean two of your easy days are easier than previously. Keep your second speed session, and your medium length run to maintain a well-balanced week.

Start this modified program at least twelve weeks before the race. You could increase your mileage of course, adding the 20 percent over the first month and maintaining that level for eight weeks. But do distribute those extra miles to the best effect.

Avoid doing any session more than three times during the 12 weeks. Alternate the key session between long, short, and hill reps.

The three to six seconds per mile slower pace during a 12K, should make you more relaxed than in the rush of 10K. You should feel you are cruising and in control.

Clearly, an increase in training should bring you better races. But if you are already training at full effort (for your body), to prepare for the 10K, you will have the speed and strength to run a good 12K.

> Running Speed at Maximum Oxygen Use (RSMO) measures how efficiently you use oxygen. It is the same speed as your 100 percent VO2 max.

Racing at 10 Miles and 15K.

Your fifteen mile run most weeks should have given you sufficient base to run an excellent 10 mile race. You trained at this race pace while following the advice in Chapter Three, but trained four to five miles at a time. You will start the race with fresh legs, so if you run the first few miles of a 15K race 10-15 seconds slower than in a 10K race, while thinking about all those tempo runs at this pace, the first five miles will feel easy. Then use your strength and economical running action to power those rested legs through the second half. This essay, from Running Dialogue pages 246-248, sums up my feelings.

OUR WORLD RECORD

The gun is fired. I'm with Kirui as we set off at world record pace: We all are. No matter which part of the pyramid of running ability you occupy, you're as much a part of his world record as he is. Eight or twenty-eight minutes behind him, we take pride in our performances. So here's the clean version of my thoughts.

As the mile marker approaches, I realize I'm having an out of skin experience with 5:10 showing on my watch -- only 45 seconds behind the leaders -- but I'm working just as hard. Maybe if I did more 400s in 62 seconds I'd be able to stay with the leaders; maybe if I could run one 62 second 400 I'd at least be closer to them.

The second mile slows to a 5:15 suggesting I didn't start excessively fast, merely a little too fast. I'm surrounded by fellows who will run this pace for several more miles, and already catching those who went too hard in the first mile. The lead group is only another 42 seconds up on us, so in a way we're already closing the gap.

Ah, the third mile, we're really rolling now; same time as the last, but the leaders repeat also. The eight 5,000 meter races this year which resulted in a 16 second PR improvement, have taught my quads to expect discomfort early, but I don't feel anything yet...What a difference 15 seconds per mile makes.

I'm sat behind a group of five runners...if sitting is an appropriate expression at eleven miles per hour. The leaders are lounging at thirteen mph of course.

Five seventeen is not unexpected as I wait for my group to weaken. The twenty times 300 meters with a 100 jog ten days ago passes through my mind. That and many similar sessions free me of fear at four miles due to the speed endurance and aerobic capacity which I've developed.

The five by 1,500 and eight by 1,000 sessions which I alternate, naturally cross my mind as we head for half-way in 26:18. The 5:21 gives another 48 seconds to the leaders, but they're welcome to it. My skin, and the skin of many others running at 6, 7 and 8 minute miles continues fairly sloughing off as we roll toward likely personal records.

Oh, the race is nearly over: get ready to sprint. Or I could if it was a 10K instead of a 10 mile race. At least it's not 10K pace...anymore. It was very close to 10K pace for a few miles, but now we will pay the price. 5:26 is not too high a price -- three years ago it would have been unheard of for me to run so fast -- yet now it represents a slowing.

I don't have a recent six mile session to help me through this mile, so I think of all the rest I've had this week. The leisurely, flat 12 instead of a hilly 14 at the weekend; three times a mile instead of the usual five midweek; and doing only two speed sessions this week has left my legs feeling fresh. It's good to reap the reward of the hardest type of training: rest.

I share the pace now as the "group" is down to two. We chase some dying runners whose positive splits will make our positive splits look positively negative. And the 5:30 mile is the most positive mile we will do today.

Each mile from here I'm thinking about my running form even more than usual. Extending the ankles and working the calves to full contraction. Whipping the leg through a little closer to the buttock to decrease the pendulum drag and increase cadence. Picking up the knees just a little more to devour the ground. And, leaning forward a micro degree, to ensure the energy propels me forward, rather than upwards with more hang-time than Michael Jordan. Hang-time is bad for distance running.

We storm towards the eight mile mark. Like the fourth thousand of the 5,000, it's the make or break section of the race for personal records. I cheat: pretending it's only an eight mile race as the legs begin to scream at me to slow -- but instead of surging at seven and a half, I merely extend the effort into the ninth mile. Chasing down other competitors also helped us to a 5:23; a mere 44 seconds slower than the winner.

Now it's the penultimate mile.

Don't gather yourself for the finishing flourish, give it all now. If you have a sprint at the end, you obviously didn't run the first nine and a half miles hard enough. Picking off runners as we reverse the slowing from mid-race, my endorphin numbered legs carry me through a 5:21 mile -- surely we're catching the leaders at this speed.

At some stage in the last mile, those who didn't run hard enough earlier come screaming by. No matter. I've run *my* legs off. I'm slowing just a little, yet I'm still catching a few. With 600 meters to go I try an extended sprint for the finish. My increase in pace is so devastating, that two of the guys at my side take 10 meters out of me in a hundred...and will be 50 ahead by the finish. Did they run hard enough in the prior 15,490 meters?

Kirui got his world record, and many went sub sixty and sub seventy minutes for the first time; due in part to a superb 5:25 last mile, I slashed my PR to 53:23. Positive splits yes, but still a very positive race.

20K and the Half-Marathon.

My third running book will be about Marathon Training, with a special chapter devoted to racing the Half.

Runners who have done 8-10 fifteen mile runs, plus hills, threshold and VO2 max pace running should be in shape to race a decent half-marathon. If weekly mileage is over 50, an eighteen mile run at 9, 6 and 3 weeks prior to the Half will improve the ability to process fats for energy and perhaps increase your aerobic capacity and leg strength. It may improve your half-marathon time; it should at least make the distance feel more manageable.

Want more Half-Marathon advice. Get a jump on my next book by looking up my three web pages starting at: http://home.sprynet.com/sprynet/holtrun/halfmara.htm

An Alternative way to Begin Running.

You could start a running program with VO2 max training, avoiding Chapters One-Three, but it will probably lead to early overtraining injuries.

Running four times a week with sessions such as: 30-40 sprints, 20-30 times 200 meters, 15 times 300 meters, and 12 times 400 meters, without a single easy run has been used by many runners during their early stages of running. Most of these runners either:

Become injured with shin splints or Achilles problems within three months, or simply lose interest because they are running gut busting sessions on zero base endurance. That is, they hurt at mile pace every time they run.

Or, they learn to canter at easy pace for 7-10 miles between each more modest paced interval session: they slow their speed sessions down to 5K pace.

Lots of 100s and 200s can build a base and leg strength quite rapidly. To race well at all distances you still need a base from some source. Threshold pace and hill running is exhilarating. Your anaerobic threshold limit is also a better predictor of race performance than VO2 max. It is prudent to work on both factors during race preparation.

Now, choose the training schedule which best fits your appetite. Adjust it as needed.

CHAPTER SEVEN

Schedules for 20 miles per week.

Phase One: Base Mileage.

How long is a long run?

You'll need to run longer than race distance to build endurance for 5K or 10K racing. At this level, you should run about 40 percent of your miles as one run-- which gives you an 8 miler. Run it at only 60 percent of your maximum heartrate (HR) to make sure it's not too grueling.

Of course, this only leaves you 12 miles for the rest of the week. Three runs of 3-5 miles will do nicely; one of which should be fartlek as described in Chapter One.

If you are new to running, start with a walk and run session; alternate one to three minutes of each until you're comfortable with the running. Add a minute or two to your running every 3-5 days.

Find the running speed which feels natural to you and you'll be less likely to get hurt. Your body may desire 75 percent of max HR to feel comfortable. Work on one aspect of your form at a time; becoming a smooth, graceful runner takes practice.

Schedules for 20 miles per week.

Here's your likely schedule.

Day 1: Long, gentle run. Add a half mile each week
until you reach eight.

Day 3: 4 miles easy, but ease up toward 70 percent of
maximum heartrate.

Day 4: 4 miles--including fartlek of various lengths and
intensities.

Day 6: 4 miles as on day 3.

Days 2, 5 and 7: Rest

Those of you wishing to train more intensely could do a
second fartlek session on Day 6.

Phase Two: Hills and Strength.

As alluded to in Chapter Two, how seriously you take
your running will dictate how often you run hills in this
phase. At the serious running end you will alternate hills
with the fartlek session on day four...running hills once
every 2 weeks, or once every 8 training runs. At
moderate intensity you'll add a hill session every week,
plus retain one of the fartlek sessions.

At the upper extreme you could keep both fartleks, while
adding the hills.

Take care of the Achilles, increase the number of hill
reps sensibly, and do 10 weeks with the emphasis on
hills for the best results.

Retain the 8 miler as the cornerstone of your aerobic
endurance. You might add other strength workouts from
Chapter Two.

Here is how your week could look.

Day 1: Long and gentle...increasing toward 70 percent
of max heartrate once you've done several eights.

Day 3: 4 miles easy, but try a couple of miles at close to
75 percent of maximum heartrate.

Day 4: 4 miles--including fartlek of various lengths and
intensities.

Day 6: 4 miles--with one mile of hill repeats--or 5
percent of your average weekly mileage.

And, of course, three rest days.

Phase Three: Anaerobic Threshold.

15K pace running is the key to strength endurance. 15K
pace is much easier to maintain than 10K pace, yet it is
just as beneficial--even more beneficial considering how
rested your legs will be compared to running at 10K
pace.

The serious trainer will simply replace the hills or fartlek
with one quality threshold session a week for 6 weeks.
Or, run a hilly fartlek one week, with a threshold pace
run the other week...for 8-10 weeks.

The moderate intensity person will run two quality sessions per week, alternating fartlek with hills on day four,
while running threshold pace on day six.

The low mileage person with highest intensity would
maintain both of the quality runs from phase 2, but ADD
the threshold pace run.

For all of you, Chapter Three guidelines allow 10 percent
of your miles to be at 15K pace, or two miles. Four times

half a mile; three times 1,000 meters; two times one mile; or, a continuous two mile run--give a nice four week rotation. Start at 80 percent max heartrate, and increase the pace over several weeks to 85 and possibly 90 percent of max HR. These percentages should have you running 10-20 seconds per mile slower than your best recent 10K race.

Here's your schedule at the high intensity end.

Day 1: Long and gentle 8 miles, staying at 70 percent of max heartrate now that you've become used to it.
Day 3: 5 miles--including 2 at anaerobic threshold.
Day 4: 3 miles--with a mile of fartlek.
Day 6: 4 miles--retain the one mile of hill repeats--or 5 percent of your mileage
Days 2, 5 and 7 are rest days.

Phase Four: VO2 Maximum Training.

Two mile race pace or 5K pace training adds power to your legs and improves the amount of oxygen you can process--and therefore your speed potential.
As always, you have several options.
The serious trainer will simply replace the anaerobic threshold session, which had been a hill session, with the VO2 pace intervals.
The second level person who runs moderately hard twice a week can rotate hills, hilly fartlek and threshold pace

runs on day three, while running VO2 on day 6 for 6-8 weeks.

The highest intensity 20 mile per week person would retain two of the three quality speed sessions from phase three each week, but ADD the VO2 max session.

The three week rotation would look like this:

Week one:
Day 1: No change...8 miles at 70 percent of max HR to maintain base aerobic ability.
Day 3: 4 miles--including 2 at anaerobic threshold.
Day 4: 4 miles--including a mile of fartlek.
Day 6: 4 miles--with 4 x 200 meters, then, 3-4 x 400 meters to get used to your 5K VO2 max pace.

Week two:
Day 1: Cruise 8 miles at 70 percent of max HR.
Day 3: 4 miles--including 2 at anaerobic threshold.
Day 4: 4 miles--with one mile of hill repeats--5 percent of your mileage.
Day 6: 8 times 300 meters at 2 mile pace.

Week three:
Day 1: Run 8 miles at 70 percent of max HR.
Day 3: 4 miles--including one mile of hill repeats
Day 4: 4 miles--with a mile or two of fartlek.
Day 6: 4 x 600 meters at 5K pace.
Then run another rotation of days three and four over the next three weeks. On day 6, run sessions of 6-8 times

Schedules for 20 miles per week.

400 meters; 10 times 300 meters; and, 5 times 600 meters. The 600s should probably be at 5K pace; the 300s at 2 mile pace. The 400s can be at either pace.

Phase Five: Race Peaking.

Rest and longer reps at two mile race pace combine to give extra pep to your legs, and maximize your VO2.

The serious trainer will replace the shorter intervals from phase 4 with half miles and 1,200 meter reps at two mile pace. Two sessions of each will suffice. The last session in your rest week could be 6 times 300 meters at the same pace...a very modest session. It's modest because you will have reduced your long run to 7 miles for two weeks, then to 6 miles while resting. Cutting the other two runs to 3 miles will complete the picture.

At the second level, running moderately hard twice a week, the resting up is more significant. Reduce the long run as above. Plus, decrease the day 3 hills, fartlek or threshold runs to two-thirds of the previous amounts. Run the same 800s or 1,200s, which the serious runner does, and cut down to three miles for the short runs.

The highest intensity 20 mile per week person can retain the VO2 max sessions on say day 3; then alternate hills and anaerobic threshold for two-thirds of the normal session on day 4. Run those long reps at 2 mile pace on day 6.

For two weeks:

Day 1: Cruise 7 miles at 70 percent of max HR for aerobic base.

Day 3: 4 miles--run a VO2 max session like in phase 4.

Day 4: 3.5 miles--including three quarters of a mile of hill repeats; for the second week run 1.5 miles at anaerobic threshold.

Day 6: 4 x 800 meters at two mile pace; for the second week run 3 times 1,200 meters at 5K pace.

Then for the next two weeks:

Day 1: 6 miles at 65 percent of max HR--this should feel easy.

Day 3: 3 miles--run a shorter VO2 max session similar to phase 4.

Day 4: 3 miles--including half a mile of hill repeats; the second week run three x half a mile at anaerobic threshold.

Day 6: 4 times 800 meters at two mile pace; for the second week run 2 x 1,200 meters at 5K pace.

Final week or two weeks

Day 1: 6 miles at 65 percent of max heartrate--real easy.

Day 3: 3 miles--4-5 times 400 meters at VO2 max.

Day 4: 3 miles--with very gentle fartlek...and no hills.

Day 6: 10K or 5K race, or run 2 times 1,200 meters at **two mile pace.**

If you have a second week, run six miles on day one; try 5 times 300 meters on day 3; run 2 easy miles on day 4; then race again.

Schedules for 20 miles per week.

Training table abbreviations:

E = Easy running...60-70 percent of maximum heartrate.

F = Fartlek

H = Hill reps

An = Anaerobic threshold pace...15K speed.

V = VO2 maximum pace intervals...2 mile to 5K speed.

All types of speedwork will require a warm-up and cooldown, giving you four miles of running.

All of you will rest on days two, five and seven.

Serious runners:

Day	one	three	four	six
Weeks 1-10	8E	4E	2F	4E
Weeks 11, 13...19	8E	4E	1H	4E
Weeks 12, 14...20	8E	4E	2F	4E
Weeks 21-26	8E	4E	2An	4E
Week 27	6E	3E	1.5F	RACE
Weeks 28-35	8E	4E	2V	4E
Week 36	6E	3E	1.5F	RACE
Weeks 37-38	7E	4E	1.5V	4E
Weeks 39-40	6E	3E	1.5V	3E
Weeks 41-42	6E	1.2V	2E	RACE

Once you're fully used to this mileage, you can make some of the miles more productive by adding additional resistance or speed sessions. You can become a moderate to very intense trainer by making a half mile harder every three months. By the end of the year you will have an extra two miles of quality training.

Moderate intensity runners:

Note: You can rest up a bit and run a race once every 4-6 weeks like the serious runners do.

Day	one	three	four	six
Weeks 1-10	8E	2F	4E	2F
Weeks 11-20	8E	2F	4E	1H
Wks 21, 23...29	8E	2F	4E	2An
Wks 22, 24...30	8E	1H	4E	2An
Weeks 31,34,37	8E	2F	4E	2V
Weeks 32,35,38	8E	1H	4E	2V
Weeks 33,36,39	8E	2An	4E	2V
Week 40	6E	2V	3E	RACE
Week 41	7E	.75H	4E	1.5V
Week 42	7E	1.5An	4E	1.5V
Week 43	6E	1.5F	3E	1.5V
Week 44	6E	1.5An	3E	1.5V
Week 45	6E	1.2V	2E	RACE
Week 46	6E	1.2V	2E	RACE

Moderate and high intensity runners might wish to reduce the anaerobic threshold section to 6 weeks, which will allow you to peak at 40 weeks. If you came in with a solid base, the fartlek section could also be reduced by 4 weeks.

Janos Ronaszeki, a deciple of Hungarian coach Mihaly Igloi says that, "Most people racing 10Ks should probably run 3-5 miles of repeats." So, consider resting up to peak for a track session per Chapter Six.

133

Schedules for 20 miles per week.

Highest intensity runners:

Include some races prior to the big one.

	Day	one	three	four	six
Weeks 1-10		8E	2F	4E	2F
Weeks 11-20		8E	2F	2F	1H
Wks 21, 23...29		8E	2F	1H	2An
Wks 22, 24...30		8E	2An	2F	2An
Weeks 31,34,37		8E	2F	1H	2V
Weeks 32,35,38		8E	1H	2An	2V
Weeks 33,36,39		8E	2An	2F	2V
Week 40		6E	2V	1.5F	RACE
Week 41		7E	2V	1.5An	1.5V
Week 42		7E	2V	1.5F	1.5V
Week 43		6E	2V	.75H	1.5V
Week 44		6E	1.7V	1F	1.5V
Week 45		6E	1.2V	.5F	RACE
Week 46		6E	1.2V	.5F	RACE

Don't attempt to speed up your day three VO2 reps in weeks 40-44. Practice form. Learn to relax at 2 mile to 5K race pace. The important sessions during the last weeks are the long reps at 2 mile pace.

CHAPTER EIGHT

Schedules for 30 miles per week.

Phase One: Base Mileage & Fartlek.

You can run one third to about 40 percent of your miles for your long run--which gives you 10-12 miles.

Either way, you'll have 6-7 miles for each of your three other runs. Your intensity level is dependent upon how many of those short runs are fartlek. If new to this mileage, maintain the mileage for at least 8 weeks before sprinting to:

Phase Two: Hills and Strength.

Hills every week, or every two weeks...it's your choice. Keep the long run. Take care of the Achilles, and increase the number of reps sensibly. Run at least 6 hill sessions of 1.5 miles before cruising onto:

Phase Three: Anaerobic Threshold.

15K pace running is relatively easy. You can run three miles at this level. Rotate, five times 1,000 meters; three times one mile; two times 1.5 miles; or, a con-

Schedules for 30 miles per week.

tinuous three mile run. Start at 80 percent max heartrate, and increase pace over several weeks to 85 and possibly 90 percent of max. This should be 20 seconds towards 10 seconds per mile slower than your best recent 10K race. Ten sessions will give you most of your threshold pace physiologic gains. Then stride effortlessly to:

Phase Four: VO2 Maximum Training.

You probably have 20 weeks at your new mileage by now, and will have raced two times each at 5K and 10K. 95 percent of VO2 max is that 5K pace. Increase your relaxation at speed, and the power to your legs with 5K and 2 mile pace (100 percent VO2 max) training. Three miles of reps for 6-10 weeks will give you most of your VO2 max gains. Then it's time to move economically to:

Phase Five: Race Peaking.

You still run VO2 max, but the key session is long reps: 800s to 1,200s at two mile pace. Cut down to 2.5 miles for each speed session for two weeks, then to two miles for another two weeks.

The relevant chapters have more details on these phases, or you can get the short version in Chapter Seven or Nine. Now here are you schedules.

Training table abbreviations:

E = Easy running...60-70 percent of max HR.

F = Fartlek

H = Hill reps

An = Anaerobic threshold pace...15K speed.

V = VO2 maximum pace intervals...2 mile to 5K speed.

All types of speedwork will require a warm-up and cooldown, giving you six-seven miles of running.

All of you will rest on days two, five and seven.

Serious runners.

Day	one	three	four	six
Weeks 1-10	10E	7E	3F	7E
Weeks 11, 13...19	10E	7E	1.5H	7E
Weeks 12, 14...20	10E	7E	3F	7E
Weeks 21-26	10E	7E	3An	7E
Week 27	8E	5E	2F	RACE
Weeks 28-35	10E	7E	3V	7E
Week 36	8E	5E	2F	RACE
Weeks 37-38	10E	6E	2.5V	6E
Weeks 39-40	8E	5E	2V	5E
Weeks 41-42	7E	1.5V	3E	RACE

Here's a surprise. Individuals who run greater than 40 miles per week have less coronary heart disease than very low mileage runners. Consider increasing your mileage with easy running--then change 20 percent of them to quality. Forty miles per week will take you closer to immortality.

Schedules for 30 miles per week.

Moderate intensity runners.

Note: You can rest up a bit and run a race once every 4-6 weeks like the serious runners do.

Day	one	three	four	six
Weeks 1-10	10E	3F	7E	3F
Weeks 11-20	10E	3F	7E	1.5H
Wks 21, 23...29	10E	3F	7E	3An
Wks 22, 24...30	10E	1.5H	7E	3An
Weeks 31,34,37	10E	3F	7E	3V
Weeks 32,35,38	10E	1.5H	7E	3V
Weeks 33,36,39	10E	3An	7E	3V
Week 40	8E	3V	5E	RACE
Week 41	10E	1H	6E	2V
Week 42	9E	2.5An	6E	2V
Week 43	8E	2F	5E	2V
Week 44	7E	2An	5E	2V
Week 45	7E	1.5V	4E	RACE
Week 46	6E	1.5V	4E	RACE

Moderate and high intensity runners might wish to reduce the anaerobic threshold section to 6 weeks, which will allow you to peak at 40 weeks. If you came in with solid base, the fartlek section could also be reduced by 4 weeks.

Try this pyramid session in weeks 32, 35, 38: Five times 600 meters at 5K pace; then, 5 x 400 meters at 2 mile pace; then, 5 x 200 meters at mile race pace. You'll be training at 90-110 percent VO2 max.

Highest intensity runners.
Include some races prior to the big one.

Day	one	three	four	six
Weeks 1-10	10E	3F	7E	3F
Weeks 11-20	10E	3F	3F	1.5H
Wks 21, 23...29	10E	3F	1.5H	3An
Wks 22, 24...30	10E	3An	3F	3An
Weeks 31,34,37	10E	3F	1.5H	3V
Weeks 32,35,38	10E	1.5H	3An	3V
Weeks 33,36,39	10E	3An	3F	3V
Week 40	8E	2V	2F	RACE
Week 41	10E	3V	2.5An	2V
Week 42	9E	3V	2.5F	2V
Week 43	8E	3V	1H	2V
Week 44	8E	2V	2An	2V
Week 45	7E	1.5V	1.5F	RACE
Week 46	6E	1.5V	1.5F	RACE

Don't attempt to speed up your day three VO2 reps in weeks 40-44. Practice economical running and good form. Teach yourself to feel relaxed at 2 mile to 5K pace.

CHAPTER NINE

Schedules for 40 miles per week

Phase One: Base Mileage.

How long should your run be when you are running 40 miles per week? The 40 percent rule gives you a 16 miler...more than you need for racing 5K and 10Ks. 35 percent gives you a 14 mile run. If you're new to this mileage, run it at only 60 percent of your maximum HR to make sure it's not too grueling.

This leaves you 26 miles to split between four runs...an average of 6.5. You could run three times at close to nine miles, but for most of you it will be time to advance to five runs per week. At least one run should be fartlek as described in Chapter one.

Here's your likely schedule.

Day 1: Long, gentle run. Add a half mile each week until you reach fourteen miles.

Day 2 & 5: Rest.

Day 3: 6 miles easy. Edge toward 70 percent max HR.

Day 4: 7 miles--include fartlek of various lengths and intensities.

Day 6: 6 miles as on day 3.

Day 7: 7 miles--including 4 miles of fartlek.

Phase Two: Hills and Strength.

Hill frequency dictates how seriously you take your running. At the serious running end you'll alternate hills with the fartlek session on day four...running hills once every 2 weeks, or once every 10 training runs. At moderate intensity you'll add a hill session every week, plus retain one of the fartlek sessions.

At the upper extreme you could keep both fartleks, while adding the hills.

Take care of the Achilles, increase the number of hill reps sensibly, and do 10 weeks with the emphasis on hills for the best results.

Keep the 14 miler as the cornerstone of your aerobic endurance. You might add other strength workouts from Chapter Two.

Here is how your week could look.

Day 1: Long and gentle. Increase toward 70 percent of max HR once you've done several fourteens.

Days 2 and 5: Rest

Day 3: 6 miles easy, but ease up toward 70 percent of maximum heartrate for half of it.

Day 4: 7 miles--including fartlek at various intensities.

Day 6: 6 miles easy.

Day 7: 7 miles--with two miles of hill repeats--or 5 per cent of your average weekly mileage.

Schedules for 40 miles per week.

Phase Three: Anaerobic Threshold.

15K pace running is the key to strength endurance. 15K pace is easier to maintain than 10K pace, yet it's more beneficial because your legs will be rested for other speed training.

The serious trainer will simply replace the hills or fartlek with one quality threshold session a week for 6 weeks. Or, run a hilly fartlek one week, with a threshold pace run the other week...for 8-10 weeks.

The moderate intensity person running two quality sessions per week will alternate fartlek with hills on day 4, but run threshold pace on day 6.

The 40 miles a week person with highest intensity would maintain both of the quality runs from phase 2, but ADD the threshold pace run.

For all of you, Chapter Three guidelines allow 10 percent of your miles to be at 15K pace, or four miles. Six times 1,000 meters; four times one mile; two times two miles; or, a continuous four mile run--give a nice four week rotation. Start at 80 percent max HR, and increase the pace over several weeks to 85 and possibly 90 percent of max. These percentages should keep you 15 seconds per mile slower than your best recent 10K race.

A book sub-titled "The Running Pyramid", should contain more than one pyramid session--see page 103. Here's another which fits perfectly at this level.

Run 2 x one mile at 15K pace, then two half miles at 10K pace, and finish with four quarters at 5K pace. Like the reps at page 66-67, this session prepares you for VO2 training; it eases you up to 5K pace.

Here's your schedule at the high intensity end.

Day 1: Long and gentle 14 miles, staying at 70 percent
of max HR now that you've gotten used to it.

Day 2: Rest

Day 3: 7 miles--including 4 at threshold pace.

Day 4: 6 miles--with 3-4 miles of fartlek--easy fartlek
for the first few weeks.

Day 5: Rest

Day 6: 7 miles--with two miles of hill repeats--or 5 percent of your average weekly mileage.

Day 7: Easy 6 miles.

Phase Four: VO2 Maximum Training.

Two mile race pace or 5K pace training adds power to
your legs and improves the amount of oxygen you can
process--and therefore your speed potential.

As always, you have several options.

The serious trainer will simply replace the anaerobic
threshold session, which had been a hill session, with
the VO2 pace intervals.

The second level person who runs moderately hard
twice a week can rotate hills, hilly fartlek and threshold
pace runs on day three, while running VO2 max on day
six for 6-8 weeks.

The highest intensity 40 mile per week person would
retain two of the three quality speed sessions from
phase three each week, but ADD the VO2 max session.

All runners can rest or cross-train on days 2 and 5.

Schedules for 40 miles per week.

The three week rotation would look like this:
Week one:

Day 1: No change...14 miles at 70 percent of max HR to maintain base aerobic ability.

Day 3: 7 miles--including 4 at anaerobic threshold.

Day 4: 6 miles--including 3-4 miles of fartlek.

Day 6: 7 miles--with 6 x 200 meters; then, 7-8 x 400 meters to get used to your 5K VO2 max pace.

Day 7: Easy 6 miles.

Week two:

Day 1: Cruise 14 miles at 70 percent of max HR.

Day 3: 7 miles--including 4 at anaerobic threshold.

Day 4: 6 miles--run two miles of hill repeats.

Day 6: 7 miles--with 12 x 300 meters at 2 mile pace.

Day 7: Easy 6 miles.

Week three:

Day 1: Run 14 miles at 70 percent of max HR.

Day 3: 7 miles--including two miles of hill repeats.

Day 4: 6 miles--with 3-4 miles of fartlek.

Day 6: 8 x 600 meters--at 5K pace.

Day 7: Easy 6 miles.

Then run another rotation of days three and four over the next three weeks. On day 6, run sessions of 12-16 times 400 meters; 15 times 300 meters; and, 10 times 600 meters. The 600s should probably be at 5K pace; the 300s at 2 mile pace. The 400s can be at either pace.

Pyramid Session.

Here is a second pyramid session, for use between phase 4 and 5 to stimulate your VO2 max:

Two times one mile at 5K race pace; then,

Two times half a mile at 2 mile pace; and finish with,

Four quarters at mile pace. Rest intervals will be longer than the session on page 142.

Phase Five: Race Peaking.

Rest and longer reps at two mile race pace combine to give extra pep to your legs, while maximizing your VO2 capacity.

The serious trainer will replace the shorter intervals from phase 4 with half miles and 1,200 meter reps at two mile pace. Two sessions of each should suffice. The last session in your rest week could be 12 times 300 meters at the same pace...a very modest session. It's modest because you will have reduced your long run to 12 miles for two weeks, then to 10 miles while resting. Cutting the other two runs to 5 miles will complete the picture.

At the second level, running moderately hard twice a week, the resting up is more significant. Reduce the long run as above. Decrease the day 3 hills, fartlek or threshold runs to two-thirds of the previous amounts. Run the same 800s or 1,200s, which the serious runner does, and cut down to five miles for the short runs.

The highest intensity 40 mile per week person can retain the VO2 max sessions on day 3; then alternate hills and anaerobic threshold running for two-thirds of

Schedules for 40 miles per week.

the normal session on day 4. Run those long reps at 2 mile pace on day 6.

On day seven, run five easy miles for the first two weeks, then four miles each remaining week.

For two weeks:

Day 1: Cruise 12 miles at 70 percent max HR for base.

Day 3: 7 miles--run a VO2 max session like in phase 4.

Day 4: 5 miles--run 1.5 miles of hill repeats; run three miles at anaerobic threshold for the second week.

Day 6: 6 times 800 meters at two mile pace; for the second week run 5 x 1,200 meters at 5K pace.

Then for the next two weeks:

Day 1: 10 miles at 65 percent max HR--should be easy.

Day 3: 6 miles--run your usual, but shorter VO2 max session similar to phase 4.

Day 4: 5 miles...including one mile of hill repeats; the second week run 5 x 1,000 meters at anaerobic threshold.

Day 6: 8 times 800 meters at two mile pace; the second week run 4 x 1,200 meters at 5K pace.

Final week or two weeks:

Day 1: 10 miles at 65 percent of max heartrate--run real easy.

Day 3: 5 miles--8 to 10 times 400 meters at VO2 max.

Day 4: 4 miles--with very gentle fartlek--and no hills.

Day 6: 10K or 5K race, or run 4 x 1,200 meters at **two mile pace;**

If you have a second week, run 10 miles on day one; try 10 times 300 meters on day 3; run 4 easy miles on day 4; then race again.

Training table abbreviations:

E = Easy runs...60-70 percent of maximum heartrate.

F = Fartlek

H = Hill reps

An = Anaerobic threshold pace...15K speed.

V = VO2 maximum pace intervals...2 mile to 5K speed.

All types of speedwork will require a warm-up and cooldown, giving you about seven miles of running.

All of you will rest on days two and five.

Serious Runners:

	Day one	three	four	six
Weeks 1-10	14E	6E	4F	6E
Weeks 11, 13...19	14E	6E	2H	6E
Weeks 12, 14...20	14E	6E	4F	6E
Weeks 21-26	14E	6E	4An	6E
Week 27	10E	5E	3F	RACE
Weeks 28-35	14E	6E	4V	6E
Week 36	10E	5E	3F	RACE
Weeks 37-38	12E	6E	3V	6E
Weeks 39-40	11E	4E	3V	5E
Weeks 41-42	10E	2.5V	4E	RACE

Day seven will be your additional six mile run.

Schedules for 40 miles per week.

Moderate Intensity Runners:

Note: You can rest up a bit and run a race once every 4-6 weeks like the serious runners do.

Day	one	three	four	six
Weeks 1-10	14E	4F	6E	4F
Weeks 11-20	14E	4F	6E	2H
Wks 21, 23...29	14E	4F	6E	4An
Wks 22, 24...30	14E	2H	6E	4An
Weeks 31,34,37	14E	4F	6E	4V
Weeks 32,35,38	14E	2H	6E	4V
Weeks 33,36,39	14E	4An	6E	4V
Week 40	10E	3V	5E	RACE
Week 41	14E	1.5H	6E	3V
Week 42	13E	3An	6E	3V
Week 43	12E	3F	5E	3V
Week 44	12E	3An	5E	3V
Week 45	10E	2V	4E	RACE
Week 46	10E	2V	4E	RACE

Day seven will be your additional six mile run.

Looking for a change of pace? Try a longer session of reps at 10K pace once a month. 400s at 90 percent of VO2 max is an extremely relaxing way to take a break from 5K pace running. You can get good endurance training by doing more reps than you would at 3K or 5K pace. Run 5 miles instead of 4 miles. See page 113.

Highest Intensity Runners:

Include some races prior to the big one.

Day	one	three	four	six
Weeks 1-10	14E	4F	6E	4F
Weeks 11-20	14E	4F	4F	2H
Wks 21, 23...29	14E	4F	2H	4An
Wks 22, 24...30	14E	4An	4F	4An
Weeks 31,34,37	14E	4F	2H	4V
Weeks 32,35,38	14E	2H	4An	4V
Weeks 33,36,39	14E	4An	4F	4V
Week 40	10E	4V	3F	RACE
Week 41	14E	4V	3An	3V
Week 42	13E	4V	1.5H	3V
Week 43	12E	4V	3An	3V
Week 44	12E	3.3V	2F	2.7V
Week 45	10E	2V	1F	RACE
Week 46	10E	2V	1F	RACE

Don't attempt to speed up your day three VO2 reps in weeks 40-44. Practice form. Feel relaxed at 2 mile to 5K pace. The key session at the end is the long reps on day six.

Moderate and high intensity runners might wish to reduce the anaerobic threshold section to 6 weeks, which will allow you to peak at 40 weeks. If you came in with a solid base, the fartlek section could also be reduced by 4 weeks.

CHAPTER TEN

Schedules for 50 miles per week.

The relevant chapters have more details on these phases, or you can get the short version in Chapter Nine or Eleven.

Phase One: Base Mileage & Fartlek.

Ha ha, fifteen miles is now only 30 percent of your mileage, and leaves you 35 to spread among your four other runs. Your intensity level depends upon how many of those 8-9 mile runs are fartlek. Of course, you could spread the fifty over six days by running an easy five instead of a rest day. If new to this mileage, maintain the mileage for at least 8 weeks before sprinting to:

Phase Two: Hills and Strength.

Hills every week, or every two weeks...it's your choice. Keep the long run. Take care of the Achilles, and increase the number of reps sensibly. Run at least 6 hill sessions of 2.5 miles before cruising onto:

Phase Three: Anaerobic Threshold.

15K pace running is relatively easy. You can run five miles at this level. Rotate, eight times 1,000 meters; five times one mile; two times 2.5 miles; or, a continuous four mile run, followed by relaxed 400s. Start at 80 percent max heartrate, and increase pace over several weeks to 85 and possibly 90 percent of max. This should be 20 seconds towards 10 seconds per mile slower than your best recent 10K race. Ten sessions will give you most of your threshold pace physiologic gains. Then stride effortlessly to:

Phase Four: VO2 Maximum Training.

You probably have 20 weeks at your new mileage by now, and will have raced two times each at 5K and 10K. 95 percent of VO2 max is that 5K pace. Increase your relaxation at speed, and the power to your legs with 5K and 2 mile pace (100 percent VO2 max) training. Five miles of reps for 6-10 weeks will give you most of your VO2 max gains. Then it's time to move economically to:

Phase Five: Race Peaking.

You still run VO2 max, but the key session is long reps: 800s to 1,200s at **two mile pace**. Cut down to 4 miles for each speed session for two weeks, then to 3 miles for another two weeks.

Schedules for 50 miles per week.

Training table abbreviations:
E = Easy runs...60-70 percent of maximum heartrate.
F = Fartlek
H = Hill reps
An = Anaerobic threshold pace...15K speed.
V = VO2 maximum pace intervals...2 mile to 5K speed.
All types of speedwork will require a warm-up and cooldown, giving you about nine miles of running.
All of you will rest on days two and five.

Serious runners.

Day	one	three	four	six
Weeks 1-10	15E	9E	5F	8E
Weeks 11, 13...19	15E	9E	2.5H	8E
Weeks 12, 14...20	15E	9E	5F	8E
Weeks 21-26	15E	9E	5An	8E
Week 27	12E	5E	3F	RACE
Weeks 28-35	15E	9E	5V	8E
Week 36	12E	5E	3F	RACE
Weeks 37-38	14E	9E	4V	8E
Weeks 39-40	12E	5E	3V	6E
Weeks 41-42	10E	2.5V	5E	RACE

Day seven will be your additional six mile run.

Moving to moderate or high intensity is simple--replace one mile of steady running with one mile of quality or faster running every 2-3 months. After one year you will have given yourself 4-5 extra miles of resistance, threshold or VO2 max training.

152

Moderate intensity runners.

Note: You can rest up a bit and run a race once every 4-6 weeks like the serious runners do.

Day	one	three	four	six
Weeks 1-10	15E	5F	9E	5F
Weeks 11-20	15E	5F	9E	2.5H
Wks 21, 23...29	15E	5F	9E	5An
Wks 22, 24...30	15E	2.5H	9E	5An
Weeks 31,34,37	15E	5F	9E	5V
Weeks 32,35,38	15E	2.5H	9E	5V
Weeks 33,36,39	15E	5An	9E	5V
Week 40	12E	3V	6E	RACE
Week 41	15E	2H	8E	4V
Week 42	14E	4An	8E	4V
Week 43	14E	4F	6E	4V
Week 44	13E	3An	6E	3V
Week 45	10E	2.5V	5E	RACE
Week 46	10E	2.5V	5E	RACE

Day seven will be your additional six mile run.

Moderate and high intensity runners might wish to reduce the anaerobic threshold section to 6 weeks, which will allow you to peak at 40 weeks. If you came in with solid base, the fartlek section could also be reduced by 4 weeks.

153

Schedules for 50 miles per week.

Highest intensity runners.

Include some races prior to the big one.

	Day	one	three	four	six
Weeks 1-10		15E	5F	9E	5F
Weeks 11-20		15E	5F	5F	2.5H
Wks 21, 23...29		15E	5F	2.5H	5An
Wks 22, 24...30		15E	5An	5F	5An
Weeks 31,34,37		15E	5F	2.5H	5V
Weeks 32,35,38		15E	2.5H	5An	5V
Weeks 33,36,39		15E	5An	5F	5V
Week 40		12E	4V	3F	RACE
Week 41		15E	5V	4An	4V
Week 42		14E	5V	2H	4V
Week 43		13E	5V	3An	4V
Week 44		12E	3.3V	3F	3V
Week 45		12E	2.5V	2F	RACE
Week 46		12E	2.5V	2F	RACE

Day seven will be your additional six mile run.

Don't attempt to speed up your day three VO2 reps in weeks 40-44. Practice good running form. Feel at ease and relaxed at 2 mile to 5K pace. The key session toward the end is the long reps on day six (or seven if you choose to run them the day before your long run).

CHAPTER ELEVEN

Schedules for 60 miles per week.

Phase One: Base Mileage

Your fifteen mile run is now only 25 percent of your weekly miles. The other forty-five miles is a lot to play with. Easy days will be nine or ten miles, which will help your fifteen to increase your aerobic capacity. Run most at only 60 percent of your maximum heartrate (HR) if you're new to this mileage.

Your speed sessions will be six miles, making 9-10 miles with the warm-up. At least one run should include 6 miles of fartlek as described in Chapter One.

Here's your likely schedule:

Day 1: Long, gentle run. Add a half mile each week until you reach fifteen, then maintain that mileage for another 10 weeks before moving on to hill training.

Day 2: 8 miles easy

Day 3: 10 miles easy, but ease up toward 70 percent of maximum heartrate for the middle 3 or 4 miles.

Day 4: 10 miles--with 6 miles of fartlek.

Day 5: 7 miles easy

Day 6: Rest

Day 7: 10 miles--including 6 miles of fartlek.

Schedules for 60 miles per week.

Phase Two: Hills and Strength.

Hill frequency dictates how seriously you take your running. At the serious running end you'll alternate hills with the fartlek session on day four...running hills once every 2 weeks, or once every 12 training runs. At moderate intensity you'll add a hill session every week, plus retain one of the fartlek sessions.

At the upper extreme you could keep both fartleks, while adding the hills.

Take care of the Achilles, increase the number of hill reps sensibly, and do 10 weeks with the emphasis on hills for the best results.

Keep the weekly 15 miler and the easy eights as the cornerstone of your aerobic endurance. You might add other strength workouts from Chapter Two.

Here is how your week could look.

Day 1: Long and gentle...increase toward 70 percent of max HR now that you've done several fifteens.

Day 2: Easy 8 miles

Day 3: 10 miles easy, but ease up toward 75 percent of maximum HR for half of it.

Day 4: 10 miles--including 6 miles of fartlek. Run a variety of distances and intensities.

Day 5: Easy 8 miles

Day 6: Rest

Day 6: 9 miles--with three miles of hill repeats--or 5 percent of your average weekly mileage.

Phase Three: Anaerobic Threshold.

15K pace running is the key to strength endurance. 15K pace is easier to maintain than 10K pace, yet it's more beneficial because your legs will be rested for other speed training.

The serious trainer will simply replace the hills or fartlek with one quality threshold session a week for 6 weeks. Or, run a hilly fartlek one week, with a threshold pace run the other week...for 8-10 weeks.

The moderate intensity person running two quality sessions per week will alternate fartlek with hills on day four, but run threshold pace on day six.

The 60 miles a week person with highest intensity would maintain both of the quality runs from phase 2, but ADD the threshold pace run.

For all of you, Chapter Three guidelines allow 10 percent of miles to be at 15K pace, or six miles. Six miles as a continuous run is quite a challenge; most coaches suggest four mile tempo runs. However, you can break the six miles down to reps of: ten times 1,000 meters; six times one mile; three times two miles; or, two times three miles. The longer reps should dominate. The miles in particular are relaxing during phase five. Start at 80 percent max heartrate, and increase the pace over several weeks to 85 and possibly 90 percent of max. These percentages should keep you running 10-20 seconds per mile slower than your best recent 10K race.

A book sub-titled "The Running Pyramid", should contain more than one pyramid session--see page 103. This next pyramid session is perfect for 60 mile weeks.

Schedules for 60 miles per week.

Run two x 1.5 miles at 15K pace, then three half miles at 10K pace, and finish with six quarters at 5K pace. Like the reps at page 66-67, this session prepares you for VO2 training; it eases you up to 5K pace.

Here's your schedule at the high intensity end.
Day 1: Long and gentle 15 miles, staying at 70 percent of max HR now that you've become used to it.
Day 3: 10 miles--with 6 miles of threshold intervals.
Day 4: 8 miles--including 5 miles of fartlek--easy fartlek for the first few weeks.
Day 7: 7 miles--with three miles of hill repeats--or 5 percent of your average weekly mileage.
Days 2 and 5 will be easy eight mile runs.

Phase Four: VO2 Maximum Training.
Two mile race pace or 5K pace training adds power to your legs and improves the amount of oxygen you can process--and therefore your speed potential.

As always, you have several options.

The serious 60 mile a week trainer will simply replace the anaerobic threshold session, which had been a hill session, with the VO2 pace intervals.

The second level person who runs moderately hard twice a week can rotate hills, hilly fartlek and threshold pace runs on day three, while running VO2 max on day six for 6-8 weeks.

The highest intensity 60 mile per week person would retain two of the three quality sessions from phase three each week, but ADD the VO2 max session.

The three week rotation would look like this:
Week one:

Day 1: No change...15 miles at 70 percent of max HR to maintain base aerobic ability.

Day 3: 9 miles--including 6 at anaerobic threshold.

Day 4: 8 miles--run 4-5 miles of fartlek.

Day 7: 8 miles--with 8 x 200 meters, then, 8-10 x 400 meters to get used to your 5K VO2 max pace.

Easy 10 mile runs on two restive days will give more endurance than running a seven on all three rest days.

Week two:

Day 1: Cruise 15 miles at 70 percent of max HR.

Day 3: 9 miles--including 6 at anaerobic threshold.

Day 4: 7 miles--run three miles of hill repeats.

Day 7: 8 miles--with 16 x 300 meters at 2 mile pace

Plus two ten mile runs.

Week three:

Day 1: Run 15 miles at 70 percent of max HR.

Day 3: 7 miles--including three miles of hill repeats.

Day 4: 9 miles--run 5-6 miles of fartlek.

Day 7 : 10 x 600 meters--5K pace like two weeks ago.

Then run another rotation of days three and four over the next three weeks. On day 7, run sessions of 14-20 times 400 meters; 20-25 times 300 meters; and, 12-15 times 600 meters. The 600s should probably be at 5K pace; the 300s at 2 mile pace. The 400s can be at either pace.

Schedules for 60 miles per week.

Pyramid Session.
Here is a second pyramid session, for use between
phase 4 and 5 to stimulate your VO2 max:
Three times one mile at 5K race pace; then,
Three times half a mile at 2 mile pace; and finish with,
Six quarters at mile pace.
Rest intervals will be longer than the page 158 session.

Phase Five: Race Peaking.

Rest and longer reps at two mile race pace combine to
give extra pep to your legs, while maximizing your
VO2 capacity.

The serious trainer will replace the shorter intervals
from phase 4 with half miles and 1,200 meter reps at
two mile pace. Two sessions of each should suffice.
The last session in your rest week could be 12 times
300 meters at the same pace...a very modest session.
It's modest because you will have reduced your long
run to 12 miles for two weeks, then to 10 miles while
resting. Cutting the two other runs to 5-7 miles will
complete the picture.

At the second level, running moderately hard twice a
week, the resting up is more significant. Reduce the
long run as above. Plus, decrease the day 3 hills, fartlek
or threshold runs to two-thirds of the previous amounts.
Run the same 800s or 1,200s, which the serious runner
does, and cut down to five miles for the short runs.

The highest intensity 60 mile per week person can
retain the VO2 max sessions on day 3; then alternate
hills and anaerobic threshold pace for two-thirds of

your normal session on day 4. On day 7, run those 2 mile pace long reps on fresh legs.

For two weeks:
Day 1: Cruise 14 miles at 70 percent max HR for base.
Day 3: 8 miles--run 5 miles at VO2 max as in phase 4.
Day 4: 6 miles...including 2 miles of hill repeats; the second week run four miles at your anaerobic threshold.
Day 7: 8 times 800 meters at two mile pace; for the second week run 6 x 1,200 meters at 5K pace.
Plus run two additional easy sevens.

Then for the next two weeks:
Day 1: 12 miles at 65 percent max HR--should be easy.
Day 3: 7 miles--run your usual, but shorter VO2 max session similar to phase 4.
Day 4: 6 miles--run 2 miles of hill repeats; rotate with 6 x 1,000 meters at anaerobic threshold.
Day 7: 8 times 800 meters at two mile pace; for the second week run 5 x 1,200 meters at 5K pace.
Plus two easy sixes.

Final week or two weeks
Day 1: 12 miles at 65 percent of max heartrate--run real easy.
Day 3: 5 miles--8 to 10 times 400 meters at VO2 max.
Day 4: 4 miles--with a mile of gentle fartlek--no hills.
Day 7: 10K or 5K race, or run 4 x 1,200 meters at **two mile pace**;

Schedules for 60 miles per week.

If you have a second week, try 10 times 300 meters on day 3; run a short fartlek on day 4; then race again.

Training table abbreviations:
E = Easy runs...60-70 percent of maximum heartrate.
F = Fartlek
H = Hill reps
An = Anaerobic threshold pace...15K speed.
V = VO2 maximum pace intervals...2 mile to 5K speed.
All types of speedwork will require a warm-up and cooldown, giving you 8-9 miles of running.

Serious Runners:
Run 8-10 miles on days two and four.

Day	one	three	five	seven
Weeks 1-10	15E	10E	6F	10E
Weeks 11, 13...19	15E	10E	3H	10E
Weeks 12, 14...20	15E	10E	6F	10E
Weeks 21-26	15E	10E	6An	10E
Week 27	12E	7E	4F	RACE
Weeks 28-35	15E	10E	6V	10E
Week 36	12E	7E	4F	RACE
Weeks 37-38	15E	10E	4V	10E
Weeks 39-40	12E	7E	3V	8E
Weeks 41-42	12E	2.5V	4E	RACE

Moderate Intensity Runners:

Note: You can rest up a bit and run a race once every 4-6 weeks like the serious runners do.
Run 8-10 miles on days two and four.

Day	one	three	five	seven
Weeks 1-10	15E	6F	10E	6F
Weeks 11-20	15E	6F	10E	3H
Wks 21, 23...29	15E	6F	10E	6An
Wks 22, 24...30	15E	3H	10E	6An
Weeks 31,34,37	15E	6F	10E	6V
Weeks 32,35,38	15E	3H	10E	6V
Weeks 33,36,39	15E	6An	10E	5V
Week 40	12E	4V	7E	RACE
Week 41	15E	2.5H	10E	5V
Week 42	14E	5An	10E	4V
Week 43	13E	4F	8E	4V
Week 44	12E	3An	7E	3V
Week 45	10E	2.5V	5E	RACE
Week 46	10E	2.5V	5E	RACE

Moderate and high intensity runners might wish to reduce the anaerobic threshold section to 6 weeks, which will allow you to peak at 40 weeks. If you came in with a solid base, the fartlek section could also be reduced by 4 weeks.

Schedules for 60 miles per week.

Highest Intensity Runners:

Include some races prior to the big one.
Run 8-10 miles on days two and four.

Day	one	three	five	seven
Weeks 1-10	15E	6F	10E	6F
Weeks 11-20	15E	6F	6F	3H
Wks 21, 23...29	15E	6F	3H	6An
Wks 22, 24...30	15E	6An	6F	6An
Weeks 31,34,37	15E	6F	3H	6V
Weeks 32,35,38	15E	3H	6An	6V
Weeks 33,36,39	15E	6An	6F	6V
Week 40	12E	4V	4F	RACE
Week 41	15E	6V	6An	4.5V
Week 42	14E	6V	2.5H	4V
Week 43	13E	5V	4An	3.5V
Week 44	12E	4V	4F	3V
Week 45	12E	3V	2F	RACE
Week 46	12E	2.5V	2F	RACE

Don't attempt to speed up your day three VO2 reps in weeks 40-44. Practice form. Feel at ease at 2 mile to 5K pace. The key session for the last few weeks is long reps on day seven.

If you've reached 60 miles per week, don't add another mile at easy pace because it will give you minimal strength increase. Improve your endurance by adding more reps to your speedwork. Add the extra mile as quality...16 x 100 during an easy run, or an extra mile to your threshold or VO2 max session. Make the extra mile count.

CHAPTER TWELVE

Schedules for 70 miles per week.

Phase One: Base Mileage & Fartlek.

Fifteen miles is not a challenge these days; you'll have 55 for the rest of the week. Run a twelve midweek for endurance. Add a five mile run once a week, and you'll have the same basic schedule as the 60 a week person, but with an extra mile on your speed sessions. Your intensity level depends upon how many of those 8-9 mile runs are fartlek. If new to this mileage, maintain the mileage for at least 8 weeks before sprinting to:

Phase Two: Hills and Strength.

Hills every week, or every two weeks...it's your choice. Keep the long run. Take care of the Achilles, and increase the number of reps sensibly. Run at least 6 hill sessions of 3.5 miles before cruising onto:

Phase Three: Anaerobic Threshold.

15K pace running is relatively easy. You can run seven miles at this level. Rotate, seven times one mile; 3-4 times 2 miles; or, a continuous four mile run, followed by a two mile. Start at 80 percent max HR--increase pace over several weeks to 85 and possibly 90 percent of max. This should be 20 seconds towards 10 seconds

Schedules for 70 miles per week.

per mile slower than your best recent 10K race. Ten sessions will give you most of your threshold pace physiologic gains. Then stride effortlessly to:

Phase 4: VO2 Maximum Training.

You probably have 20 weeks at your new mileage by now, and will have raced two times each at 5K and 10K. 95 percent of VO2 max is that 5K pace. Increase your relaxation at speed, and the power to your legs with 5K and 2 mile pace (100 percent VO2 max) training. Seven miles of reps for 6-10 weeks will give you most of your VO2 max gains. Unless your name is Zatopek, you will not need to run this session six days a week for a month to get ready for a race. It's just once a week. Then it's time to move economically to:

Phase 5: Race Peaking.

You still run VO2 max, but the key session is long reps: 800s to 1,200s at **two mile pace**. Cut down to 5.5 miles for each speed session for two weeks, then to 4 miles for another two weeks.

Think these seven mile speed sessions will get you injured? The greatest predictor of injury is mileage, not the amount of speedwork. Don't waste these extra miles.

Soreness is from micro muscle fiber tears...which will heal. After healing, you will have stronger muscles...if you give them sufficient rest.

The relevant chapters have more details on these phases, or you can get the short version in Chapter Eleven or Thirteen. Now here are you schedules.

Training table abbreviations:

E = Easy runs...60-70 percent of maximum heartrate.
F = Fartlek
H = Hill reps
An = Anaerobic threshold pace...15K speed.
V = VO2 maximum pace intervals...2 mile to 5K speed.
All types of speedwork will require a warm-up and cooldown, giving you 9-10 miles of running.

Serious runners.

Run 8-10 miles on days two and four.

Day	one	three	five	seven
Weeks 1-10	15E	12E	7F	10E
Weeks 11, 13...19	15E	12E	3.5H	10E
Weeks 12, 14...20	15E	12E	7F	10E
Weeks 21-26	15E	12E	7An	10E
Week 27	12E	8E	5F	RACE
Weeks 28-35	15E	12E	7V	10E
Week 36	12E	8E	5F	RACE
Weeks 37-38	15E	12E	5V	10E
Weeks 39-40	12E	7E	4V	8E
Weeks 41-42	12E	3V	4E	RACE

Schedules for 70 miles per week.

Moderate intensity runners.

Note: You can rest up a bit and run a race once every 4-6 weeks like the serious runners do.
Run 8-10 miles on days two and four.

Day	one	three	five	seven
Weeks 1-10	15E	7F	12E	7F
Weeks 11-20	15E	7F	12E	3.5H
Wks 21, 23...29	15E	7F	12E	7An
Wks 22, 24...30	15E	3.5H	12E	7An
Weeks 31,34,37	15E	7F	12E	7V
Weeks 32,35,38	15E	3.5H	12E	7V
Weeks 33,36,39	15E	7An	12E	6V
Week 40	12E	5V	8E	RACE
Week 41	15E	3H	12E	5V
Week 42	14E	5An	10E	4V
Week 43	14E	5F	8E	4V
Week 44	13E	4An	7E	4V
Week 45	12E	3V	6E	RACE
Week 46	10E	3V	6E	RACE

Moderate and high intensity runners might wish to reduce the anaerobic threshold section to 6 weeks to peak at 40 weeks. If you came in with solid base, the fartlek section could also be reduced by 4 weeks.

The more you train, the more important good form is for reducing your injury potential; it also improves your use of the limited oxygen supply. The best mechanical efficiency for you--generally smooth running--equates to faster races and fewer injuries.

Highest intensity runners.
Include some races prior to the big one.
Run 8-10 miles on day three, 12 on day four.

	Day one	two	five	seven
Weeks 1-10	15E	7F	10E	7F
Weeks 11-20	15E	7F	7F	3.5H
Wks 21, 23...29	15E	7F	3.5H	7An
Wks 22, 24...30	15E	7An	7F	7An
Weeks 31,34,37	15E	7F	3.5H	7V
Weeks 32,35,38	15E	3.5H	7An	7V
Weeks 33,36,39	15E	7An	7F	6V
Week 40	12E	5V	5F	RACE
Week 41	15E	7V	6An	5V
Week 42	14E	6V	3H	5V
Week 43	13E	5V	5An	4V
Week 44	12E	5V	5F	4V
Week 45	12E	3V	3F	RACE
Week 46	12E	3V	3F	RACE

Don't attempt to speed up your day three VO2 reps in weeks 40-44. Practice economical running form. Feel relaxed at 2 mile to 5K pace. The key session for the last few weeks is the long reps on day seven.

CHAPTER THIRTEEN

Schedules for 80 miles per week.

Phase One: Base Mileage

Your fifteen mile run is a pleasant jaunt at this level. You may be tempted to run an occasional 18, but there is no real need. The other sixty-five miles will give you plenty of aerobic base. Easy days will be up to ten miles twice a week. The big change could be your midweek run, which many runners will increase to 12 miles. Stay mostly at 60 percent of your maximum heartrate (HR) if you're new to this mileage.

Your speed sessions will be up to eight miles, making 11-12 miles with the warm-up. Serious runners at this level will run fast at least twice a week. The most intense trainers will run fast 4-6 times per week. Many of these will be 5-6 mile runs with three miles of gentle fartlek. You'll only do the 6-8 miles of speedwork 2-3 times per week. It's 8 miles of fartlek as described in Chapter One for this phase.

Think this speedwork will get you injured? The most reliable predictor of injury is mileage, not the quantity of speedwork. Don't waste these miles.

Here's your likely schedule:

Day 1: Long, gentle run. If you feel the psychological need for an eighteen mile run once every three weeks, remember to take it easy the next day. When you are used to your new mileage, maintain that mileage for another 10 weeks before moving on to hill training.

Day 2: AM 6 miles...including 30-40 strides.
PM 10 miles easy, but ease up toward 70 percent of maximum heartrate for the middle 4-5 miles.

Day 3: 11 miles--include 7-8 miles of fartlek of various lengths and intensities.

Day 4: 12 miles easy

Day 5: AM 6 miles...including 3 miles fartlek.
PM 10 miles easy, but ease up toward 70 percent of maximum heartrate for the middle 4-5 miles.

Day 6: Rest

Day 7: 11 miles--including 7-8 miles of fartlek.

Note that you only have two days with double runs, and you still have one non-running day.

Do you need ten weeks at each phase?

If you've been at this mileage before, if you think your base is solid, the fartlek section and anaerobic threshold phase could be reduced to six weeks. This will allow you to peak at 36 weeks.

Schedules for 80 miles per week.

Phase Two: Hills and Strength.

Hill frequency dictates how seriously you take your running. At the serious running end you'll alternate hills with the fartlek session on day three or seven...running hills once every 2 weeks. At moderate intensity you'll add a hill session every week, and retain the long fartlek session.

At the upper extreme you could keep both fartleks, while adding hills every 4-5 days.

Take care of the Achilles, increase the number of hill reps sensibly, and do 10 weeks with the emphasis on hills for the best results.

Keep the weekly mileage at 80 for your aerobic endurance. You might add other strength workouts from Chapter Two.

Here is how your week could look.

Day 1: Long and gentle...increasing toward 70 percent of max heartrate now that you've become used to the extra mileage.

Day 2: 10 miles easy, but ease up toward 75 percent of maximum heartrate for half of it.

Day 3: 11 miles--including 8 miles of fartlek. Use a variety of distances and intensities.

Day 4: Easy 12 miles

Day 5: Same as day 3

Day 6: Rest

Day 7: 9 miles--with four miles of hill repeats--or 5 percent of your average weekly mileage.

Don't forget those morning fartleks or strides twice a week for the extra mileage.

Phase Three: Anaerobic Threshold.

15K pace is important for strength endurance, and is easier to maintain than 10K pace, yet it improves your threshold level just as much as 10K pace does. However, your legs will be fresher for other speedwork.

The serious runner replaces one hill or fartlek session with 8 miles of threshold pace running for 6 to 8 weeks. The moderate intensity person who runs three quality sessions per week will keep the fartlek and hills while adding the 15K pace training.

The 80 miles or more person with highest intensity may run quality on four days. Change one of those sessions to threshold pace.

One way to increase your intensity...Change one easy mile to a quality mile every month for eight months.

For all runners, Chapter Three guidelines allow 10 percent of your mileage to be at 15K pace. Most coaches recommend four mile tempo runs. You can break your 8 miles to reps of: eight times one mile; four times 2 miles; or, two times 3 miles, plus a 2 mile rep. The longer reps should dominate. The mile reps are very relaxing during phase five. Start at 80 percent max HR, and increase pace over several weeks to 85 and possibly 90 percent of max HR. These percentages

Schedules for 80 miles per week.

should keep you running 10-20 seconds per mile slower than your best recent 10K race.

Here's your schedule at high intensity.

Day 1: Long and gentle 15 miles, staying at 70 percent of max HR is not easy the day after an eight mile speed session.
Day 2: AM 6 miles including three of easy fartlek.
   PM Easy ten miles.
Day 3: 8 miles--with four miles of hill repeats--or 5 percent of your average weekly mileage.
Day 4: 12 miles easy.
Day 5: AM Easy 6
   PM 10 miles--include 7-8 miles of fartlek--easy fartlek for the first few weeks.
Day 6: Rest
Day 7: 10 miles--include 8 miles of threshold intervals.

Phase Four: VO2 maximum training.

Two mile race pace or 5K pace training adds power to your legs and improves the amount of oxygen you can process--and therefore your speed potential.
As always, you have several options.
The serious athlete who runs moderately hard twice a week can rotate hills, hilly fartlek and threshold pace runs on day three, while running eight miles of VO2 max on day six for 6-8 weeks. With years of running background, eight miles at 5K pace should not be a

huge challenge. It will take many weeks before you gain full benefit from these sessions.

Unless your name is Zatopek, you will not need to run this session six days a week for a month to get ready for a race. It's just once a week.

The higher intensity 80 mile per week person would retain two of the three quality speed sessions from phase three each week, but ADD the VO2 max session.

The three week rotation would look like this:

Week one:

Day 1: No change...run 15 miles each week at 70 percent of max HR to for base aerobic ability.

Day 3: 10 miles--including 8 at anaerobic threshold.

Day 4: 10 miles--including 7-8 miles of fartlek.

Day 7: 11 miles--with 12 x 200 meters, then, 14 x 400 meters to get used to your 5K VO2 max pace.

Do easy 10 mile runs and fartleks on your two restive days to maintain your mileage.

Week two:

Day 3: 10 miles--including 8 at anaerobic threshold.

Day 4: 8 miles--run four miles of hill repeats.

Day 7: 8 miles--with 25 x 300 meters at 2 mile pace.

Week three:

Day 3: 8 miles--including four miles of hill repeats.

Day 4: 10 miles--with 7-8 miles of fartlek.

Day 7: 15 x 600 meters--use the same pace as two weeks ago.

Schedules for 80 miles per week.

Then run another rotation of days three and four over the next three weeks. On day 7, run sessions of 25 times 400 meters, plus a dozen 200s; 25-30 times 300 meters, plus a couple of half miles; and, 15-20 times 600 meters. The 600s should probably be at 5K pace; the 300s at 2 mile pace. The 400s can be at either pace.

Phase Five: Race Peaking.

The rest, combined with longer reps at two mile race pace, give extra pep to your legs, while maximizing your VO2 capacity.

The serious trainer will replace the shorter intervals from phase 4 with half miles and 1,200 meter reps at two mile pace. Two sessions of each should suffice. The last session in your rest week could be 15 times 300 meters at the same pace...a very modest session. It's modest because you will have reduced your long run to 12 miles for two weeks, then to 10 miles while resting. Cutting the total mileage to 60 for two weeks, then to 45 will complete the picture.

At the second level, running moderately hard twice a week, the resting up is more significant. Reduce the long run. Decrease the day 3 hills, fartlek or threshold runs to two-thirds of previous amounts. Run the 800s or 1,200s, and cut easy runs to seven, then five miles.

The highest intensity 80 mile per week person can switch the VO2 max sessions to day 3; then alternate hills and anaerobic threshold runs for two-thirds of your normal session on day 4. On day 7, run those long reps at 2 mile pace on fresh legs.

For two weeks:
Day 1: Cruise 14 miles at 70 percent max HR for base.
Day 3: 10 miles--run 6 miles at VO2 max as in phase 4.
Day 4: 7 miles...including 3 miles of hill repeats;
    the second week run six or seven miles at your anaerobic threshold.
Day 7: 10 times 800 meters at two mile pace; for the second week, run 7 x 1,200 meters at 5K pace.
Plus two easy tens and two short fartleks.

Then for the next two weeks:
Day 1: 12 miles at 65 percent max HR--should be easy.
Day 3: 7 miles--run your usual, but shorter VO2 max session similar to phase 4.
Day 4: 6 miles--including 2.5 miles of hill repeats;
    second week run 5 x mile at anaerobic threshold.
Day 7: 10 times 800 meters at two mile pace; for the second week, run 6 x 1,200 meters at 5K pace.
Plus two easy sevens, and two 2 mile fartleks in the mornings.

Final week or two weeks
Day 1: 12 miles at 65 percent of max HR--real easy.
Day 3: 5 miles--8-10 times 400 meters at VO2 max.
Day 4: 4 miles--with a mile of very gentle fartlek--and no hills.
Day 7: 10K or 5K race, or run 4 x 1,200 meters at two mile pace;

Schedules for 80 miles per week.

If you have a second week, try 12 times 300 meters on day 3; run a short fartlek on day 4; then race again.

Training table abbreviations:

E = Easy runs...60-70 percent of maximum heartrate.
F = Fartlek
H = Hill reps
An = Anaerobic threshold pace...15K speed.
V = VO2 maximum pace intervals...2 mile to 5K speed.
All types of speedwork will require a warm-up and cooldown, giving you 10-12 miles of running.

Serious runners.

Day	one	three	five	seven
Weeks 1-10	15E	12E	8F	5F
Weeks 11, 13...19	15E	12E	4H	5F
Weeks 12, 14...20	15E	12E	8F	5F
Weeks 21-26	15E	12E	8An	5F
Week 27	12E	5F	8E	RACE
Weeks 28-35	15E	12E	8V	5F
Week 36	12E	4F	7E	RACE
Weeks 37-38	15E	12E	6V	5F
Weeks 39-40	12E	7E	4V	3F
Weeks 41-42	12E	3V	4E	RACE

Note the 12 on day three and the modest fartlek session on day seven. Days two and four will be easy tens, plus gentle fartleks during a six mile run.

Moderate intensity runners.

Note: You can rest up a bit and run a race once every 4-6 weeks like the serious runners do.

Run 10 miles easy and a short fartlek session on day two; run 30 strides and an easy ten on day five; run an easy 12 miles on day four.

Day	one	three	seven
Weeks 1-10	15E	8F	8F
Weeks 11-20	15E	8F	4H
Wks 21, 23...29	15E	8F	8An
Wks 22, 24...30	15E	4H	8An
Weeks 31,34,37	15E	8F	8V
Weeks 32,35,38	15E	4H	8V
Weeks 33,36,39	15E	8An	6.5V
Week 40	12E	4V	RACE
Week 41	15E	3.5H	6V
Week 42	14E	7An	5V
Week 43	13E	6F	5V
Week 44	12E	5An	4V
Week 45	10E	3V	RACE
Week 46	10E	2V	RACE

During weeks 40 to 45, decrease the daily mileage for days two, four and five by 1-2 miles per week. Weekly mileage should be at 65 by week 43, and at 50 toward the end.

Schedules for 80 miles per week.

Higher intensity runners:

Intensity depends on how many of your sixes and easy runs you run as fartlek or strides, and how consistently you run the eight mile speed sessions.

Day	one	three	five	seven
Weeks 1-10	15E	8F	5F	8F
Weeks 11-20	15E	8F	8F	4H
Wks 21, 23...29	15E	8F	4H	8An
Wks 22, 24...30	15E	8An	8F	8An
Weeks 31,34,37	15E	8F	8An	8V
Weeks 32,35,38	15E	4H	8F	8V
Weeks 33,36,39	15E	8An	4H	6.5V
Week 40	12E	4V	5F	RACE
Week 41	15E	3.5H	8V	6V
Week 42	14E	7An	3H	5V
Week 43	13E	6F	7V	5V
Week 44	12E	5An	5F	4V
Week 45	10E	3V	3E	RACE
Week 46	10E	2V	5E	RACE

Don't attempt to speed up your day three VO2 reps in weeks 40-44. Practice form. Feel at ease at 2 mile to 5K pace. The key session for the last few weeks is the long reps at 2 mile pace on day seven.

Running 100 miles or more per week.

I won't use another 10 pages by adapting the prior few pages to meet the higher mileage runners.

The schedules on page 178 to here are more than adequate for the 120 mile per week runner.

Schedules for 80-120 miles per week.

You simply need to fit in an extra fartlek or a 70 percent of maximum HR run on most days. You might run 10 percent of your mileage as a single speed session, but you're more likely to restrict yourself to about 8 miles of reps.

According to early quotes as Running Pyramid goes to press, Ronaldo Da Costa of Brazil does 15 times 1,000 meters in 3:01. That's much slower than his half marathon race pace; barely anaerobic threshold. However, his recoveries were only 20-30 seconds.

It's a similar story for his VO2 max session. Twenty-five times 400 meters in 66-68 seconds is not demanding for a 28 minute 10K runner--unless the recoveries are only 15-20 seconds.

Twelve months after his first marathon, Da Costa took 3 minutes off his marathon PR, and 45 seconds off the world best, in his second race at the distance. At 28, Da Costa may be at his peak. His ten plus years of hard training have paid off.

The sensible use of bulky, yet modest paced intervals, and high mileage, may help to lower your 10K and 5K times. Only time and consistency of training will enable you to find out how fast *you* can race on high mileage.

So, add a mile to your repeats once a month until you reach 10 miles at 15K pace.

Add an 800 and 400 each month until you reach 10 miles at 5K pace.

Add extra mileage cautiously. Do moderate amounts of cross training. Include several types of resistance training. If you rest up once a month to race, within 12 months you should see significant progress.

Pace Charts.

The **Anaerobic Threshold** pace chart and user guide are on pages 69 and 70. Fifteen K race pace develops your strength endurance.

The **VO2 Maximum Training** pace chart for 5K and 2 mile speeds is on pages 91 and 92. VO2 training builds additional leg strength and improves running economy.

This **Speed Chart for Even Paced PRs** gives your goal or split times for the main distances which you'll race. Practice pace judgment with long reps at race pace. Run more than ten seconds too fast for the opening mile of a 5K or 10K race, and you will probably suffer. Even pace is better.

8:00	**16:00**	**24:51**	**40:00**	**49:43**	**59:39**	**1:14:34**	**1:20:00**	**1:44:53**
8:15	16:30	25:38	41:15	51:16	61:31	1:16:54	1:22:30	1:48:09
8:30	17:00	26:24	42:30	52:49	63:23	1:19:13	1:25:00	1:51:26
8:45	17:30	27:11	43:45	54:22	65:15	1:21:33	1:27:30	1:54:42
9:00	**18:00**	**27:58**	**45:00**	**55:55**	**67:06**	**1:23:53**	**1:30:00**	**1:57:59**
9:30	19:00	29:31	47:30	59:02	70:50	1:28:33	1:35:00	2:04:32
10:00	20:00	31:04	50:00	62:08	74:34	1:33:12	1:40:00	2:11:06

Even Pace Running Chart.

MILE TIME	2 miles	5k 3.1m	5 m	10k 6.21m	12k 7.46m	15k 9.32m	10 miles	13.1 miles
4:50	9:40	15:01	24:10	30:02	36:03	45:03	48:20	1:03:52
5:00	10:00	15:32	25:00	31:04	37:17	46:36	50:00	1:05:33
5:10	10:20	16:03	25:50	32:06	38:31	48:09	51:40	1:07:58
5:20	10:40	16:34	26:40	33:08	39:46	49:42	53:20	1:09:55
5:30	**11:00**	**17:05**	**27:30**	**34:10**	**41:01**	**51:15**	**55:00**	**1:12:06**
5:40	11:20	17:36	28:20	35:12	42:16	52:48	56:40	1:14:17
5:50	11:40	18:07	29:10	36:14	43:30	54:21	58:20	1:16:28
6:00	**12:00**	**18:39**	**30:00**	**37:17**	**44:44**	**55:56**	**60:00**	**1:18:39**
6:10	12:20	19:10	30:50	38:19	45:59	57:29	1:01:40	1:20:50
6:20	12:40	19:41	31:40	39:22	47:14	59:03	1:03:20	1:23:01
6:26		20:00		40:00		60:00		
6:30	13:00	20:12	32:30	40:24	48:28	1:00:36	1:05:00	1:25:13
6:45	13:30	20:58	33:45	41:57	50:20	1:02:55	1:07:30	1:28:29
7:00	**14:00**	**21:45**	**35:00**	**43:30**	**52:12**	**1:05:15**	**1:10:00**	**1:31:46**
7:15	14:30	22:31	36:15	45:03	54:04	1:07:34	1:12:30	1:35:03
7:30	15:00	23:18	37:30	46:36	55:55	1:09:54	1:15:00	1:38:19
7:45	15:30	24:05	38:45	48:09	57:47	1:12:14	1:17:30	1:41:36

FURTHER READING

Galloway's Book on Running by Jeff Galloway.
Running Injury Free by Joe Ellis D.P.M. Rodale Press.
Run Fast by Hal Higdon...training for the 5 and 10K.
The Runner's Coach by Roy Benson.
Running with the Legends by Mike Sandrock.
The Loneliness of the Long Distance Runner by Alan Sillitoe.
The Olympian by Brian Glanville.
The Runner's Literary Companion...Running related essays, editor Garth Battista.
Better Training for Distance Runners, by David Martin and Peter Coe...Leisure Press
Competitive Runner's Training Book. Bill Dillenger and Bill Freeman...Macmillan.
Daniels' Running Formula by Jack Daniels PhD.
Train Hard, Win Easy, Training the Kenyan way, by Toby Tanser.
Kenyan Running by John Bale.
Running Dialogue...How to Train...5K to the Marathon. Serious content presented in a light hearted way; includes cartoons, humorous essays, nutrition and extensive injury advice, by David Holt.
Many are available from Cedarwinds Publishing
1-(800)-548-2388
Magazines--**Running Times**...1-(800) 816-4735
Runner's World...1-(800) 666-2828
Information--American Running and Fitness Association
9310 Old Georgtown Road, Bethesda, MD 20814
Road Runners Club of America (RRCA)
1150 S. Washington St. # 250, Alexandria, VA 22314

Mail your orders to David Holt
   PO Box 543, Goleta, CA 93116
Or E-mail   holtrun@sprynet.com
Payment by check or Visa, Mastercard, Discover
Card or Check Number..........................
Name on card.........................Expires on.............
Send books to:......................................
   Street..
   City & State...
   Telephone..............................

Copies

10K & 5K Running, Training & Racing:
The Running Pyramid, 180 pages,
ISBN 0-9658897-1-8...$17.95   ....
Running Dialogue: Humorous How to Train
5K to Marathon, with Nutrition and Injury
advice, 280 pages, ISBN 0-9658897-4-2..$17.95 ......
   add shipping of $3:05 for each copy   ....
Add sales tax of 7.75 % (of book price) if to
California address, $1:39 per running book   ......

From May 9th, the year 2,000 also at $17.95
Marathon Running, Training & Racing:
The Marathon Pyramid, ISBN 0-9658897-3-4 ....

Retribution, The novel. ISBN 0-9658897-2-6
Divorce attorney kidnapped and interrogated.
Divorcees changing the divorce system to get
attorneys out of the divorce business. $14:95 plus
$2:05 shipping = $17.00 (+CA Tax $1.16)   ....
                                    Total......

At bookstores or the Internet stores please use the
ISBN number. Have bookstores call the Distributors
at (219) 232-8500

Multi Copy Discounts.

2 copies of 10K & 5K Running, Training & Racing: $35.00 includes shipping and tax.
http://home.sprynet.com/sprynet/holtrun/10krun.htm

2 Copies of Running Dialogue: $35.00 including shipping and tax.
One copy of each...also $35.00
http://home.sprynet.com/sprynet/holtrun/

Any three running books...$50.00 includes shipping and tax.

Please don't order **Marathon Running, Training & Racing:** The Marathon Pyramid, ISBN 0-9658897-3-4 until *May 9th 2,000.*
Price will be $17.95 per copy plus shipping and tax.
http://home.sprynet.com/sprynet/holtrun/marathon.htm

Want David's novel too?
Retribution, The novel. ISBN 0-9658897-2-6
Divorce attorney kidnapped and interrogated. Divorcees getting attorneys out of the divorce business. Add it to a pair of running books for $12:00, including shipping and tax.
For all these books you can use the Internet stores. Or have your local bookstore call the Distributors at (219) 232-8500. Please use the ISBN numbers.

Order Blank.
Mail your orders to David Holt
   PO Box 543, Goleta, CA 93116
Or E-mail   holtrun@sprynet.com
Payment by check or Visa, Mastercard, Discover
Card or Check Number..........................
Name on card.........................Expires on............
Send books to:.....................................
   Street..
   City & State...
   Telephone..............................

Name of Book
Number of copies
Running books are $17.95 plus $3.05 shipping,
Add $1.39 tax if to California.

Order Blank.

Mail your orders to David Holt
   PO Box 543, Goleta, CA 93116
Or E-mail   holtrun@sprynet.com
Payment by check or Visa, Mastercard
Card or Check Number...........................
Name on card..........................Expires on.............
Send books to:......................................
   Street..
   City & State..
   Telephone...............................

Name of Book
Number of copies
Running books are $17.95 plus $3.05 shipping =
$21.00
Add $1.39 tax if to California.